ADVANCE PRAISE

"Defining Wealth for Women marries brain science and the sordid history of women and money to empower women with the tools they need to create wealth."
—Farnoosh Torabi, host of podcast *So Money* and author of *When She Makes More*

"Bonnie Koo is calling for a 'women's wealth revolution,' and her book Defining Wealth for Women is going to kickstart that revolution. Her book beautifully marries science with strategy and offers the tools every woman should master to become wealth-empowered. This is a must-read for any woman who desires peace, purpose, and plenty of cash!"
—Amy Porterfield, host of the podcast *Online Marketing Made Easy*

"Many financial experts view money as if it's a math problem with an easy formula, setting women up for frustration when the formula doesn't work. Dr. Koo takes us for a non-jargon stroll through the brain's architecture and natural instincts that can trip us up on money and society's women-specific programming that piles on those instincts. Armed with the truth, we learn how to make, own, and manage our money confidently."
—Sarah Catherine Gutierrez, Founder of Aptus Financial and author of *But First, Save 10: The One Simple Money Move That Will Change Your Life*

"In many ways, women start out their financial lives with one arm tied behind their back. Dr. Koo will help you even the playing field and reach your financial dreams!"
—James M. Dahle, MD, Founder of The White Coat Investor

"If you want to learn the truth about your own money beliefs and exactly how to change them, this is a must-read."
—Natalie Bacon, JD, CFP, Founder of NatalieBacon.com

"Dr. Bonnie Koo is the voice that professional, ambitious women need to feel empowered about their money choices. She is an excellent example of someone who went from being in debt to becoming an investing powerhouse. She is a trusted voice in the personal finance space and someone many women—myself included—look up to."
—Catherine Alford, author of *Mom's Got Money: A Millennial Mom's Guide to Managing Money Like a Boss*

"This book is an invitation for women to challenge the common belief that it is taboo to talk about money. It is not only okay to talk about money but critically important for women to talk about money if we ever want to earn equal pay or have equal economic power."
—Sunny Smith, MD, Founder of Empowering Women Physicians

"Every woman needs this book. We have to start the change we want to see so that our daughters and granddaughters aren't still fighting for true financial equality and equal pay. The change starts with us at an individual level and our socialized beliefs, many of which we're unaware of, that are holding us back. Bonnie's book is a roadmap on everything you need to begin that journey. A must-read!"
—Linda Street, MD, host of the podcast *Simply Worth It*

"Women often hold themselves back from being (and feeling) wealthy. Defining Wealth for Women is for every woman ready to break that cycle."
—Letizia Alto, MD, host of the podcast *Rich Doc Poor Doc*

"This book should be required for every woman at every stage of their wealth building. Our thoughts about money are formed by multiple factors and it's about time to take control of them through the lessons taught in Defining Wealth for Women."
—Hala Sabry, DO, MBA, Founder of Physician Moms Group and Feminist Legacy Coach

"Bonnie Koo's work is so important. In a world where even highly-trained professional women earn less than their male counterparts, we have to take our financial futures into our own hands. This book will help you do just that."
—Kara Loewentheil, host of the podcast *UnF*ck Your Brain*

This book is dedicated to you.

(Your future self asked for it.)

Defining Wealth for Women:

(n.) PEACE, PURPOSE, AND PLENTY OF CASH!

BONNIE KOO, MD

LIONCREST
PUBLISHING

DEFINING WEALTH FOR WOMEN:
(n.) Peace, Purpose, and Plenty of Cash!

ISBN   HARDCOVER: 978-1-5445-2431-3
        PAPERBACK: 978-1-5445-2430-6
        EBOOK: 978-1-5445-2429-0
        AUDIOBOOK: 978-1-5445-2432-0

CONTENTS

"When women are hesitant to make money and create wealth, they usually do not understand that by opting out of the game, they are ensuring it continues to be rigged against them."

—KARA LOEWENTHEIL

"Wealth is the ability to fully experience life."

—HENRY DAVID THOREAU

INTRODUCTION

Wanting to be rich was always part of a larger story about possibility for me. I wanted something bigger—a bigger life, a bigger vision, and yes, a bigger income. Along with that itchy sense that there was more available "out there," I used to also have a strong sense of having settled. Even after I finished medical school and was making good money at a good job, I didn't really believe I could live my life the way I wanted to—on my own terms, without sacrifice or waiting until I retired to start enjoying myself.

In the spring of 2018, I was living in Philadelphia and working as a dermatologist in a private practice. It was the life I'd gone into medical school (and a lot of debt) to achieve. I wasn't loving it, but I wasn't sure anyone really loved their life. Besides, what I had was certainly good enough. I wasn't yet bringing in more than what the practice was paying me, so there was a deficit I needed to make up, but my contribution was increasing steadily. If I stayed where I was through the end of the year, I'd be making enough to pay them back and have my salary where I wanted it to be. Despite it being only seven more months, I was restless.

I didn't want to spend another three-quarters of a year just trying to get where I wanted to be. I'd always followed the prescribed path and thinking about taking a different route was scary, but I started to wonder: "What if I don't have to stay here to pay them back? What if I could pay them back some other way?" It wasn't an entirely comfortable question.

The funny thing about uncomfortable questions, though, is that they're powerful—even if you don't have answers for them. It was as if the question I'd started asking myself went out into the universe and started asking around on my behalf. And on some level, it also felt like it went to work trying to find an answer for me. Or maybe I just started paying a different kind of attention. Either way, I was browsing a *locums tenens* directory (a listing of short-term medical assignments) and stumbled across a summer post in Seattle working two weeks on, two weeks off for three months of the city's best weather. Suddenly there was a way to do something different and still pay off my debts. I jumped! I moved to Seattle, worked the job for three months, and went from there to a similar position in Hawai'i.

Living December to February in Hawai'i is so much better than it is in Philly that it broke down internal limits I didn't know I had. I'd stepped off the approved-of path and ended up on Lanikai Beach! That gave me the audacity to start verbalizing more of what I wanted my life to be. I wanted it to be bigger. I wanted a stronger sense of purpose, a deeper internal peace, and much more money. I got bolder, and I got ambitious—not just for myself, but for other successful, type-A, professional women living with that itch for more feeling like they'd settled, gotten stuck, or fallen behind.

In the same way that "rich" doesn't just mean having money, "professional" doesn't necessarily mean being rich. Still, many educated, professional women live paycheck-to-paycheck burdened with crushing debt and even heavier shame. If you feel overwhelmed by how complicated it seems to manage your finances or if you find you're constantly stressed about money, you're not alone.

HOW WE GOT HERE

Many smart, successful women scramble to make more and spend less, wondering why they don't have a better grip on it all. Other people seem to get it, but where does their confidence come from? Did you maybe miss a memo? Were you absent that day?

Maybe money wasn't something your family talked about. Maybe you're embarrassed by your debt or spending. Maybe you're dealing with uncertainty lightly dusted in shame. Whatever it may be, I can help.

I began my financial coaching career focusing on female physicians (no slouches in the intelligence or self-discipline department), and I promise, if working in the medical field was all it took to feel capable and in control of your personal finances, I would have gone back to medicine myself. If that were all it took, you probably wouldn't be reading this book.

In most parts of the world, for most of history, women have been legally barred from owning property (the primary source of wealth in preindustrial societies). From the Middle Ages until the mid-1800s, a married woman had no legal status at all. She was not an independent entity and had no individual financial rights. In 1839, Mississippi became the first state in the US to allow women to own property in their own names. By 1845, when women were first allowed to file their own patents (giving them the rights to their intellectual property), much of the rest of the country had caught up with Mississippi in property rights. The final two stragglers (Utah and South Carolina) didn't grant women "separate economy" until 1895.

Until 1963, it was legal to pay women less for the same work. After 1974, a woman no longer had to have a man cosign to take out a loan. It's been fewer than fifty years since the law of the land said women weren't responsible enough to borrow money independently. Is it any wonder many of us still struggle to trust ourselves?

Beyond the legal inequalities all women have faced for thousands of years (and the additional burdens borne by women of color), there are different social and cultural norms for men and women that are maybe even more powerful and damaging because they're less obvious. From childhood, boys get the message that they can and should create wealth while girls are socialized to rein in spending and focus on saving money.

This only gets more pronounced as we get older. Take a quick survey of the different money and finance articles on the internet targeting men or women. Men get earning and investment topics. Women get savings and fiscal restraint. Women are still getting the message that they just can't be trusted with money. Men spend; women splurge. Men make a purchase. Women go shopping. Men can take risks and be smart with money. Women need to exercise self-control and be more sensible.

Data shows that men and women over-spend equally. We're equally likely to carry consumer debt, make purchases on impulse, and buy things we don't need, but what women spend money on is deemed less worthy. A man who spends several thousand dollars on a watch will consider a pair of shoes that cost half as much a frivolous purchase. Many women have internalized this. We feel inadequate around money. We second-guess ourselves. We pathologize our spending and carry around a lot of shame.

This is the reason we need a book on wealth. We have thousands of years of history to undo, and the damage is ongoing. No matter what the Equal Pay Act promised, women are still paid less than men for the same work. We still get much more punishing messages about what it's okay to spend money on, what qualifies as over-spending, and who's allowed to do it.

A WOMEN'S WEALTH REVOLUTION

If you're feeling inadequate, overwhelmed, and stressed about money, please know that there's nothing wrong with you, and you're not alone. Too many women are afraid they're never going to get to live the life they want due to massive student loan debt or the need to "keep up with the Joneses." They are tired of being frugal. They don't know where to start learning the basics and keep trying to work harder and spend less, all the while feeling guilty for not having already figured it out or for wanting more in the first place.

We need a women's wealth revolution. As women free themselves of our unfair history and unequal messaging, and as more of us become rich, we rewrite the female financial narrative and change the rules. We can (and will!) replace the systems that keep women small. Taboos, misconceptions, and limiting beliefs conspire to keep too many women working for their money rather than having their money work for them.

In *Defining Wealth for Women*, I'll share knowledge and practices that help women realize there really are no limits on what they can earn and do. Each chapter takes on one of the common myths or misconceptions about money that are holding women back. We'll look at how the way our brains are wired gets in our way, and I'll teach you how to think differently about yourself and your finances. We'll uncover and reframe hidden, mistaken ideas and replace them with better information, history- and brain science-based explanations, and recommendations.

Each chapter starts with a self-assessment, quiz, or thought experiment and contains a "This Is Your Brain" section in which I explain why some things are so hard to do (and some, way too easy!). Finally, each chapter ends with an opportunity to turn your insights into action. Here you'll find journaling prompts and other activities designed to help you engage more deeply with the material. I've collected all these chapter-ending exercises into a PDF workbook you can download for free here: https://definingwealthforwomen.com.

By reading and engaging in this way, you'll learn powerful cognitive tools to rewire your brain so you can create wealth. But being rich isn't just about money. Sure, financial abundance is part of the story, but having real wealth means having a healthy bank balance, body, and mind—peace, purpose, and plenty of cash! We'll look at how reframing your beliefs and changing your mindset contribute to more of all three.

I haven't always known the things I'll be teaching you. I was a board-certified dermatologist with a solid career ahead of me when I started contrasting December, January, and February in Philadelphia with what passes for winter in Hawai'i. It showed me how much your unquestioned beliefs can limit the quality of your life.

When I realized that the work of identifying artificial limits, misplaced guilt, and mistaken ideas was the missing piece in money education, particularly for women, it changed everything. I felt a call to play a part in a women's wealth revolution. I left medicine and became a financial educator and coach.

As I worked with clients and watched their a-ha moments and successes, it became clear to me that, although women came to me because they had money problems, it was never really just about the money. Their financial troubles were a gateway to the changes in their thinking and beliefs that they needed to make to start living extraordinary and truly wealthy lives. I saw what may be the biggest secret paradox of wealth: having plenty of money lets you stop worrying and thinking about money and frees you up to work on what brings peace and purpose to your life.

This is my purpose. I started living it in 2019, coaching clients and creating Money for Women Physicians, an online coaching and financial literacy program. Its success has led me to move it into book form for nondoctors and other women who might not be financially able to participate in individual coaching (although I'll make a strong argument for the fiscal wisdom of such an investment in Chapter 5).

Defining Wealth for Women isn't as explicitly programmatic as my online program and workshops tailored to female physicians. Still, it will offer any professional woman both important reframing and tactical recommendations. It will help you understand and take apart the myths and misconceptions around money that are holding you back. The first may be exactly the one that brought you to this book in the first place—the belief that money is complicated.

CHAPTER 1

Myth: Money Is Complicated

Take a quick inventory of everything you're hoping to get out of this book. What motivated you to pick it up? What are your goals in reading it? Take a moment and write down your goals for our work together.

* * *

If your experience with your own finances and with what passes for financial education in schools or the media has been less than satisfying, wanting to learn more is a completely reasonable desire. Since you've picked up a book about wealth for women, you clearly hope to add to your store of knowledge about money, but trying to learn enough to untangle the complexities isn't the only (or most effective) way to increase your understanding.

There's an old expression I like: "To a man with a new hammer, everything looks like a nail." (I could rewrite a less gendered "When you have a new knife, everything looks like a steak," but most of the women I know are actually pretty good with hand tools.) If you're like most of my clients, you're an educated, type-A (or high achieving) professional woman who can attribute a great deal of your success to your education and to your ability to learn. That's your hammer. Your financial acumen, your ability to manage your finances, and your anxiety about your spending, savings, debt, and investments are the nails you picked up this book to pound flat. Fair enough. I will teach you to do all those things, but first, let's take a look at your toolbox.

THE PIE OF ALL KNOWLEDGE

Imagine a circle that represents all the knowledge in the world. You know only a fraction of it, right? A pie chart representing this idea might show a gray wedge of knowledge you already possess with the balance of the circle in black. When we learn new things, we move something from the black "unknown" to the gray "known," and we think of education and training as the best ways to move more knowledge into the "Stuff I Know" wedge.

It's not hard to stand on the border of what you already know and peer into the dark of the unknown with a good guess about what's out there. You know there are things about money you don't know. You know you don't know how to fly the space shuttle. You know you don't know Russian. You also know that, if you wanted to, you could learn these things, or at least that there are people out there who have.

In other words, there are things you know you know and things you know you don't know. But hidden inside the ter-

Pie of All Knowledge

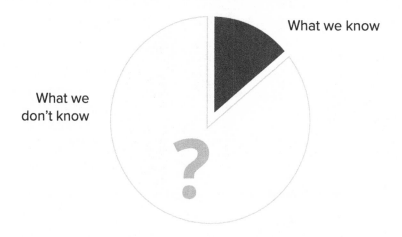

ritory of things you don't know are things you're entirely unaware of—things you don't know that you don't know.

It's a bit like living in a skyscraper knowing you've only explored the first four floors. If someone asks you what you know and don't know about your building, you'd identify the floors you're familiar with, and likely say something like, "And there are many other floors I haven't visited and don't know."

Now, imagine the floor collapses, and you discover there's a basement. You didn't know you didn't know about it. It wasn't even on the blueprints.

There are things you don't know that you don't know.

Now you have a new way of looking at buildings: they rise above the ground and descend below it. If asked about your building now, you might say something like, "There are floors

Pie of All Knowledge

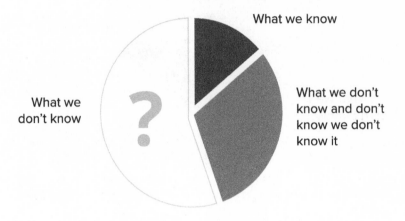

above and basement levels below me that I haven't visited and don't know," because now you know you don't know them.

When you shift from thinking the Pie of All Knowledge is divided into what you know and what you don't know—when you go from thinking your building is all above ground—you've gone from a finite to an infinite mindset.

MINDSETS

Mindsets frame how you think, not what you know—whether you think of buildings as made up of just floors or of floors and basement levels. You can learn a lot more about the floors above you without changing your mindset, but until you do, you can't learn about the basement because you don't know it's there.

Everything you think, feel, know, and do is
framed and structured by your mindset.

Mindsets are hard to think about, difficult to spot, and tricky to explain, so analogies and examples end up being our best tools. Mindsets are most often conceptualized as an internal lens or set of lenses we don't know we have but through which we see (and don't see) the world. A pessimistic mindset, for example, can literally blind a person to happy accidents, while an optimistic mindset might make people equally unable to see certain red flags. Even when optimists and pessimists see the same thing, they will explain it in different ways.

Of course, there are many degrees of optimism and pessimism. There are also many mindsets—abundance and scarcity, growth and fixed, approach and retreat, deserving and unworthy, black-or-white and shades of gray, infinite, and finite. They layer over each other, creating the many different ways in which people see and understand reality.

I graduated from medical school with about 150 people, and if you'd asked each of us what med school was like, you would probably have gotten 150 different answers. Some of this has to do with personality and ability, but most of it is mindset. Each of us has our own layered set of mindsets filtering and explaining our experience differently.

But you can change your mindset.

Changing your mindset changes your entire experience. If you have an unworthiness mindset and think you're not strong enough or disciplined enough to change it, learning that it's an option may feel like bad news. But that can change too! The thought "I don't have enough willpower to change" comes out of an "I'm unworthy" or "Something's wrong with me" mindset. If you didn't have that mindset, you wouldn't have those thoughts, and learning that you can change your mindset would sound like great news. (Which it is!)

Once you are aware that there are mental frameworks that filter and color what and how you see and understand the world and that those frameworks are different for everyone and can be changed—once you have a mindset mindset—you can start making huge improvements in your life because you no longer have to believe what you think. There is a mindset-based reason for this that I'll take you through, but first, we need to understand what thoughts are.

THOUGHTS

We have approximately sixty thousand thoughts a day, many of which we're never consciously aware of. Others show up as words in your head. Often, they're observations: "I'm tired" or plans: "I'm going to Starbucks." Sometimes, they're simply descriptive: "A guy just walked into Starbucks." More often, they're judgments: "That guy is cute." Most often, they're negative commentary: "Of course I'm wearing pajama pants the one day a cute guy walks into Starbucks." Sometimes they're downright mean: "I'm such an idiot. And he wouldn't be interested in me if I'd taken an hour getting dressed and lost ten pounds."

We know our thoughts belong to us because they're in our head, and nobody else can hear them (and thank God for that!), but because we don't know where they come from, we don't usually take the time to evaluate them. We just accept they're true. In other words, we believe our thoughts. Additionally, because we think in the first person, we think we are our thoughts. But if we are, who's that listening? Thoughts come into our awareness. We are the person who hears them. You are the person listening to the first-person voice talking in your head. And you can choose to disagree.

If I have the thought, "I look terrible," I can stop and question my thinking. Do I look terrible, or is it possible I'm just adorably rumpled? Additionally, does it matter how I look? I may be rumpled, but I'm smart! So, not only can you question your thoughts, but you can dispute them and decide to think something different.

You can train yourself to think more useful thoughts.

You can also simply disregard some thoughts. If "I'd like a coffee" pops into my head while I'm working, I can just ignore it. Having had the thought that I'd like a coffee doesn't require me to go to Starbucks. I can decide to stay at my desk.

Realizing you aren't your thoughts gives you some distance from them. I live in a high-rise building, and the window in my kitchen looks down on a constantly busy four-lane highway. In the mornings, during rush hour, when I make my first cup of tea (or coffee), I watch the cars go by—fast little ones, big loud ones. They're different colors, moving at different speeds in different lanes—far below and really, nothing to do with me. I like to watch them and remind myself that I can watch my thoughts go by with the same peaceful distance. Just as I listen to a taxi driver hitting their horn, I can also listen to a loud, insistent thought and let it go right on by.

BELIEFS

Once you've had a thought enough times, it becomes a belief, and it goes underground. You think it without even knowing it's there. It's like a given thought walks the same pathway in your mind and thinking that thought over and over wears a channel in your thinking the way feet kill off the grass through a field. After the pathway is there, it just makes sense for other thoughts to travel the same, well-worn route. Beliefs are what give us certainty about who we are and what things mean. And human beings like certainty. The desire to replace doubt with certainty is one of the driving forces that motivates many of us. In fact, to a certain extent, our lives are simply a manifestation of our beliefs.

Does that mean you're doomed to keep thinking the same thoughts even once you've recognized some of them aren't very nice and start to argue with them? Absolutely not! It's possible to unearth your deeply seated beliefs and even to deliberately change them. It's hard work, but changing one of your mindsets can be a powerful tool.

Remember, mindsets limit what you can think. If you have a scarcity mindset, the thought, "I have everything I need will simply never occur to you, much less repeat enough to become an ingrained belief. With an abundance mindset, a whole new range of thoughts becomes available.

By the time we reach our third or fourth decade, we've been thinking certain thoughts over and over for so long that they've worn a track in our minds. But a new mindset creates new beliefs.

To return to our earlier analogy, you can imagine a mindset as a box of lenses. All day long, your brain pulls lenses (thoughts) from one or more of its boxes (mindsets). A fixed mindset box will offer up thoughts like, "That's just the way I am" and "I can't change the way I was raised." A scarcity mindset will supply thoughts like, "I need more," "There's never enough," and "I'll run out" whenever your brain reaches for a thought about money.

Sometimes when I tell clients they can change their mindset or choose their thoughts, they initially have a negative emotional reaction. It seems to them that there's something inhuman about it, and they worry that it means we'll all basically turn into robots. I promise you that's not the case.

YOUR MONEY MINDSET

Imagine you're thinking about taking a vacation. Your optimistic mindset might provide thoughts about how much fun you'll have on your trip, while your scarcity mindset will offer up worries about whether you can afford it. If you have a fear mindset, it will amplify that worry-thought, and you might decide to stay home. If you have a rebellious mindset, you might decide to retaliate against your money concerns by putting first-class tickets on your credit card, knowing you can't pay them off.

A new abundance mindset would make new thoughts available. Maybe you'd realize you have plenty of money for a shorter vacation and that's really all you need. A new mindset makes new thoughts possible. It doesn't make them automatic or easy, and it doesn't happen all at once. We often need to inch our way there. I coach clients to move from scarcity to sufficiency ("I have enough right now") before reaching for abundance ("There's more than enough for everyone"). Changing your mindset isn't about moving from one pole of a dichotomy to the other, but about recognizing that new thoughts are possible. Once you internalize that, retraining your brain to think these new thoughts is like training your muscles. It's all about doing the reps.

THIS IS YOUR BRAIN

Brains like to be efficient (or lazy, if you have a slightly less charitable mindset). Your brain is the most energy-intensive organ in your body. It takes a lot of calories to think, and evolution has taught us to conserve our energy because food hasn't always been as plentiful and as available as it is today. As a species, we've spent many more years having to hunt or forage for every calorie we consume than we've spent in grocery stores, at vending machines, or in coffee shops nearby.

Today, we use our brains to do most of our work, but this is new too. For most of our evolutionary lives, our bodies have been more important to our welfare, wealth, and survival, so our brains evolved to do as little work as efficiently as possible. This means we're programmed to automate anything we can.

Beliefs are thoughts that your brain has automated because it's easier and takes less energy to spit out a quick "I'm an idiot" whenever you make a mistake than it is for it to carefully evaluate the situation and make a more nuanced judgment. Thinking new thoughts takes more energy, so your brain thinks "No thanks!" It's just doing its job when it puts up resistance to new ideas, and it doesn't care if its automatic thoughts are mean or counterproductive. All it cares about is that they're easy.

Our brains like to be efficient (a.k.a. lazy).

If your money mindset is providing you with thoughts like, "Money is complicated" and "I'll never have enough," thinking about money probably feels terrible. These aren't helpful thoughts (and you can probably recognize that), but they are efficient. Because they're familiar, easily available, and "thinkable" without much thought, your brain is literally programmed to think them. It's just doing its job, conserving energy, and spitting out the easiest thought it can find as quickly as possible.

I explained this to a client once who asked a question I hear quite often: "If our brains kick out thoughts without really thinking about them, should I just stop thinking altogether?" "No!" I told her. "Not only is that not possible, but you wouldn't want to do it anyway." Thinking is how we attach meaning to events, and that's part of what makes us human. If we didn't, we'd be robots, and nobody wants that!

FLEX YOUR MINDSET

Go back to the assessment at the beginning of this chapter. Can you see now how each one of the questions is based on the Pie of All Knowledge mindset? Because you weren't aware of how mindsets operate, you were focused on your "learning more" hammer—on moving additional knowledge from the unknown into the known portion of the circle. You were focusing on tactics, but tactics account for only 20 percent of personal finance problems. Your money mindset is responsible for the other 80.

Yes, you may need to learn new tactics and acquire more knowledge about how investing works or where wealth comes from, and I'll provide tactics and information in the chapters ahead. Still, the most powerful and effective changes you'll make won't be in what you know about money but in how you think about it. They'll be pieces of a new money mindset.

All personal finance problems are
either tactics- or mindset-based.

The tendency to focus on tactics rather than mindset isn't limited to money. It's a very human trait. Because they're lazy (and for other reasons we'll go into in the next chapter), our brains much prefer to keep using the hammer they already know.

For smart, educated, professional women, our favorite hammer is usually our intelligence and ability to learn. Sometimes, we notice its limits—you'll hear it in the questions we ask each other over drinks: "If I'm so smart, why can't I lose weight?" or "I've read all the dating books, why am I still single?" But we keep going back to the same thinking tool. Often, it serves us well. We love learning, and we're good at figuring things out, but not every problem has a rational, tactical solution. But limited mindsets limit the range of tactics and strategies that are available to you. New mindsets create new possibilities. For many of the stickiest problems, it's not what you know that's the issue; it's how you think—it's your mindset.

Moving things from the unknown into the known changes what you know. Shifting mindsets changes understanding.

A NEW DEFINITION OF UNDERSTANDING

When you become aware that there are things you don't know you don't know, you can start to see that your mindset frames, filters, and structures everything you think, feel, know, and do. This is a powerful tool for change! Improving how you think can have a much more positive impact on your life than adding to what you know.

Mindsets are based on beliefs that are, in turn, formed from often-repeated thoughts, and thoughts are just words in your head. You don't have to believe what you think. You can choose to think differently and build new mindsets that are more liberating and empowering than those you inherited from your culture, parents, and experiences. Making changes in your money mindset is what this book is all about. The myth that money is complicated is the first we tackled because it's the first standing in your way. Money isn't complicated. You don't need more information; you need a new money mindset. Once you have that, the tactics are easy to learn and implement.

TURNING INSIGHTS INTO ACTION

1. Think about the reasons you listed at the beginning of the chapter for picking up this book.
   a. Did what you learned in the chapter change your answers?
   b. How much of what you wrote down is about tactics?
2. Tune into your thoughts about money. What does that voice in your head say about money? Do you have some thoughts that might be replaced with more helpful ones? Write a few of them down.
3. What were you taught about money growing up and from whom?
4. Were you taught that money is hard and complicated? In what way?
5. Did your family talk about money? What did they say or not say?

Old Myth: Money is complicated. I need to learn more about it.

New Mindset: Money is easier than my job. I just need to think about it differently.

Not only is how you think about money more important than what you know about it, but it's also the source of unnecessary stress. We'll tackle that and how you feel about money in the next chapter.

Myth: Money (or Lack Thereof) Is Stressful

"I'm so stressed out!" is often the first thing I hear from clients when we sit down together. The reasons they give for their anxiety fall broadly into one of two categories: I don't have enough, and I don't know enough. As we learned in the last chapter, these reasons are both mindset-based. Once my clients understand that idea, we start talking about the facts of the situation they're in.

From the list below, mark the things you might say to me if I asked why you feel stressed:

I can't afford to take a vacation.
I'm broke.

I have a spending problem.

I'm bad with money.

I need a budget.

Only rich people can own assets.

My house is an asset.

Only rich people invest in real estate because it's too risky.

I can't pay off my student loan debt quickly enough.

I can't pay off my credit card debt quickly enough.

I shouldn't have credit card debt in the first place.

Credit card debt is bad debt, but even on the "good" student loan debt I have, I'm only making the minimum payment, and that's bad.

It's smart to pay off my student loans as quickly as I can

I'm not making enough.

Debt stresses me out.

The smartest investment strategy is to start early and let compound interest do all the heavy lifting.

* * *

My clients express their concerns about having enough in many different ways: They don't have enough to put a down payment on a house. They're working too many hours but don't make enough to work less. They don't have enough saved for their kids' college. Sometimes "not enough money" shows up as "too much spending." They may feel guilty about "splurging" on luxuries they can actually afford or feel sad about the vacation they're denying themselves. Sometimes they deny themselves for so long and so severely that they really do over-spend in an act of frustrated rebellion. (In Chapter 4, we'll address over-spending directly, but in this chapter, we'll talk about the umbrella issue—how you feel about money.)

WOMEN, MONEY, AND FEELINGS

Most people have at least some fear of running out of money. People with student loan debt usually worry about that as well. A divorce, job loss, or a new baby can raise stress levels to the point that they make people sick. The scarcity mentality kicks in: I don't have enough, I'll never have enough, I'll end up poor and alone and living under a bridge. (I don't know why it's always under a bridge, but it is.)

Sometimes the "I don't have enough" brand of money stress has an additional level of stress-generating guilt: "I feel like I don't have enough, but I have so much more than so many. What's wrong with me?" Plenty of people feel bad about feeling bad about their finances, but we can't "feel bad" our way out of feeling bad. Women often have an additional layer of social conditioning that contributes to their stress. If we've internalized messages about women, wealth, and greed, even financial success can be stressful. Many women feel the need to apologize for wanting to be rich. In our society, a little boy and a little girl who list "getting rich" as one of their life goals are likely to be met with different responses. The boy might be met with an indulgent but understanding chuckle, the girl with questions about why she wants to be rich or even with value judgments about wealth—that she shouldn't be greedy or that money doesn't buy happiness. Even a crack about finding a rich husband.

Women are much more likely to be challenged about their financial aspirations than men. As a friend of mine points out, nobody ever asked Bill Gates why he wanted to put a computer on every desk. Another friend of mine found, after her divorce, that people assumed her business had cost her her marriage. There's an unspoken assumption that women can't have both a successful business and a solid marriage. Spending time on one obviously detracts from the other. You can't give 100 percent to two things, after all. The same calculus isn't applied to men. I don't know whether the assumption is that a marriage doesn't need as much from men or that business success and marital success don't draw from the same well of emotional resources for men, but the idea that it's hard to make a lot of money and have a happy marriage seems to be peculiar to women.

A BAD DREAM

Imagine you woke up tomorrow morning and discovered that you had exactly $1,000. You rent your apartment, you lease your car, and in all your accounts combined, you have only $1,000. How would you feel? Probably pretty stressed, right? If I asked why, you'd probably tell me you looked at your balance, saw $1,000, and immediately felt anxious.

I know that's what it feels like, but if we could slow time down, you'd see a chronology that involves a few more steps. When you saw $1,000 in your checking account, your brain told you a story about it. Maybe it was a story that involved being hacked or robbed. Maybe it was a story about being flaky or a screw-up. Either way, it was those thoughts, not the $1,000 balance, that triggered the emotion of stress. In fact, if you think about it, you can probably remember a time when $1,000 in your bank account would have been cause for celebration.

FEELINGS

It feels like feelings are caused directly by things that happen—by circumstances in the outside world—but that isn't the case. Emotions don't just happen to us or within us. So what are they, and where do they come from?

Feelings are simply sensations you feel in your body. Emotions like fear or anxiety are often a tightness in the chest or stomach. Waves of warmth or cold, prickling on the back of the neck or in the hands, and constriction in the throat or shoulders are other ways feelings show up. We describe a feeling in terms of physical sensations, but they're subtly different from feelings of pain or heat that come from external sources because they're caused by thoughts, and thoughts are internal.

ANNIE AND RACHEL

When I was growing up, I was friends with two girls who were twin sisters. Annie was anxiety prone, got good grades, and thought a lot about trying to fit in. Rachel was happy to stand out. She was the first person I knew to dye her hair something other than blonde, red, or black. She went with blue. It was very punk.

One day, Rachel and I found Annie hiding out in the bathroom during lunch. One of the "it" girls at the school had made fun of her sweater with a sneering, "Where'd you get that, Goodwill?" Annie was humiliated. "That girl embarrassed me," she told us. Rachel didn't understand the problem. She proudly bought most of her clothes at Goodwill.

Annie's experience was very much that the girl's unkind words had caused her to feel ashamed. The same circumstance would have produced different feelings in Rachel because it isn't what was said but how she thought about it that caused Annie's feelings.

It isn't circumstances but thoughts that cause feelings.

Annie had a money mindset that put money and worthiness together. She thought because her family didn't have as much money as the other girls' families, they were somehow less than, less appropriate, and less desirable. Rachel had a money mindset that held wealth in contempt. To her, not having money made her worthier, more noble, and more real.

When Annie heard the question, "Where'd you get that, Goodwill?" her money mindset and unworthiness mindset served up thoughts like: "My clothes are wrong. They're not from Goodwill, but they're not from Abercrombie & Fitch either. I can't afford to shop there, and I never will. I look stupid and cheap, and I'll never fit in!"

In the same circumstance, Rachel's money mindset likely would not have even been triggered. She'd have answered, "Yup," and gone on about her business. (Which, of course, is why those girls only asked Annie.) In different circumstances—if, for example, blink-182 was in town—Rachel's money mindset might serve up thoughts that would trigger emotions (probably rage) just as Annie's thoughts had made her sad. The circumstances—the cruel comment or expensive tickets—are neutral. The thoughts Annie and Rachel have about them cause their sadness, anger, or indifference.

Money doesn't cause stress. Thoughts about money cause stress.

Thoughts cause feelings, but that's not how it feels. For most of us, our lived experience is quite the opposite. We have an emotional reaction, and then we think (and overthink) about it. Especially when there is a history of trauma, one of four trauma responses—fight, flight, freeze, or fawn—can take hold. The flight impulse urges you to avoid or run away from danger, while the fight response may make you respond too aggressively. The freeze reaction may make you incapable of moving (or making a choice), while fawning behaviors include people pleasing or conciliating to avoid conflict.

Trauma isn't limited to "big" events such as abuse—any event or circumstance you experienced as a child or young adult that overloaded your body or brain counts—so most people have had some by the time they reach adulthood. At the time, you created defense mechanisms to keep you safe, but as you grew up, they stuck with you and may still be "helping" you avoid feeling the negative emotions the trauma caused. Some of you may have trouble actually feeling anything at all as it requires you to pause your thinking and be in your body. If so, you're not alone! Many women I work with struggle to access their emotions. But you are not a brain in a jar. Your body is designed to feel.

Think back to the $1,000 bank balance scenario. What would you have been feeling? You probably would have been aware of your racing heart and constricting chest. Then you would have consciously thought about the problem: "What should I do? What went wrong? Why is there only $1,000 in the account?" It makes sense to believe the feeling caused the thoughts because there are two kinds of thinking, and they originate in different parts of your brain.

THIS IS YOUR BRAIN IN TWO PARTS

Different parts of your brain do different jobs. The one that makes you human is called the prefrontal cortex (also called the higher or adult brain). It's the part of you that's capable of higher-level thinking. It's responsible for planning and making the kind of decisions you make deliberately, like where to go to college and whether to start that new exercise program. That it is not the only part of you with decision-making ability is obvious when we make impulsive, in-the-moment choices that go against our rational, made-before-hand ones.

The prefrontal cortex is the most recently evolved part of your brain. We talk about it in contrast with the older, more primitive (animal, toddler, lower) parts of your brain. Your prefrontal cortex thinks all the thoughts you hear yourself thinking. Your primitive brain doesn't think in words and has only one idea: don't die! It's afraid you'll get eaten. It doesn't want you to try new things. It wants you to stay inside and keep doing only those things you've always done that haven't killed you yet.

I'm poking fun a little bit. This part of your brain did its job well for about two hundred thousand years, or you wouldn't be here today. Unfortunately, the work our animal brains have done to keep us alive long enough to reproduce and keep the species going isn't as useful today as it was when we had predators and famines to worry about. In our comfortable, modern world, certain features of this old brain aren't just less useful; they can actively get in the way. When a rustle in the bushes was once as likely to mean "thing that will eat me" as "pleasant breeze," responding with a full-alert warning made a lot of sense. Today, we're still often flooded with the same feelings that let our early ancestors run away from danger when there's nothing actually threatening our lives.

Even if the bad dream we imagined came true and you woke up one morning to find you had only $1,000 in the bank, you wouldn't actually be in immediate life-and-death danger. But it would feel that way. Your primitive brain would provide your body with all the "flight or fight" panic chemistry that tells you urgently to run or hide. This part of your brain isn't interested in logic; it's interested in speed. Speed is helpful in outrunning lions. Logic—not so much. The prefrontal cortex, in contrast, is slow and effortful. Unlike the primitive brain, it can learn new things and make thoughtful rather than instinctive decisions. It can think about thinking. It can reprogram itself. In a footrace, the primitive brain will always win, but the prefrontal cortex can outwit it. Not only that, your prefrontal cortex can overrule your primitive brain.

Like weight training, training your brain to think differently is slow and painful at first. It's also inefficient, so your brain will fight it. You're breaking down muscles and beliefs to build them back stronger and healthier. You wake up sore. You "forget" to go to the gym. But it gets easier. With enough repetition, you start thinking your new thoughts more easily and then automatically. Eventually, for the same reasons it was so hard to pick it up, your new thought becomes embedded and part of you.

FEELINGS, YOUR BRAIN, AND ACTION

When I said above that it isn't the circumstance—the thing that's happened, like seeing the $1,000 bank balance—but your thoughts about it that cause your feelings, it's true on two levels. There's the circumstance that causes the primitive brain's quick and automatic reaction to danger which, in turn, causes the feeling of fear. These feelings then cause the mindset-generated thoughts that pop into your mind, which cause another layer of emotion. And all this happens before your prefrontal cortex can get itself in gear!

Circumstance: $1,000 in the bank

Primitive brain: Danger!

Emotion: Fear

Automatic, mindset-based thought: "I'm terrible with
money."

Emotion: Shame

Feeling shame and fear isn't any fun, so your brain responds automatically again, providing you with actions to take to make the bad feelings go away. (There are four ways of responding to a feeling, and we'll discuss them in detail in Chapter 4.) In this instance, you might stop looking at your bank balance and distract yourself with some internet or refrigerator surfing. In fact, almost any action you take (or don't take) is motivated by emotion.

Your feelings are your fuel.

The actions you take—whether it's to ignore your $1,000 bank balance or to stress-eat, to call the bank in a panic, or to flip on a movie to distract yourself—all produce results. Over time and with repetition, these results become your life. They also close the loop and reinforce the thoughts that set the reaction in motion, turning your thoughts into a self-fulfilling prophecy machine. If, for example, you see that $1,000 bank balance and think, "I'm terrible with money," feel ashamed, and distract yourself from that unpleasant feeling, you won't deal with the bank balance. It will then create more circumstances that trigger your "terrible with money" thoughts and corresponding feelings of shame.

Circumstances trigger thoughts. Thoughts cause feelings.
Feelings inspire actions. Actions create results.

PUT DOWN YOUR HAMMER (AGAIN)

In the circumstance-thought-feeling-action-result sequence, the most important component is feeling, but most of my clients—educated, cerebral professionals that they are—like to focus on the thinking piece. I'm sympathetic. I'm more comfortable in the intellectual rather than the emotional space myself. As part of our training, doctors are taught to suppress or manage our emotions to such an extent that it can feel like we're not really supposed to have them at all. But here again, the "female" part of being a "female professional" plays a role.

Part of our cultural narrative about women is that we're more emotional than men. We're overly emotional, not rational, too sensitive. (For me, it's a double whammy—as a Korean-American and a woman, I'm not allowed to have any feelings at all!)

Most women who have achieved any level of professional success have learned to keep their feelings more hidden than men do—in part because stereotypically "female" emotions and ways of expressing emotion (like crying) are less acceptable and because the standard is higher for women. Men who are perfectly comfortable shouting will shut women down for tearing up. (Or shouting, for that matter.)

As a result, it can be very tempting for women to intellectualize the entire sequence and use our big brains to try and change our behaviors rather than dealing with the emotions that actually power them. It's understandable, but it's ineffective. Emotions are the energy source. We need to learn how to work with them directly.

> "Feelings are for feeling."
> —Glennon Doyle

No matter how it feels, your feelings can't kill you. They may be very intense, but they are always temporary. We may go to great lengths to avoid experiencing certain painful emotions like grief, failure, and shame, but they—and all emotions—are part of the human experience.

Often, my clients will make the mistake of thinking that if thoughts create feelings, all they need to do to feel happy all the time is choose different thoughts, but that's not the way it works. Our lives aren't made up of 100 percent positive experiences—we aren't meant to be happy all the time. We're meant to experience the full range of emotions: happy and sad, excited and bored, thrilled and disappointed. In other words, we are meant to have a human experience.

Once you understand the way events, thoughts, feelings, actions, and results relate to each other, you're able to work on each part—to coach yourself. It will help you separate what happened from what you made it mean and how your interpretations of events affect how you feel. It's a powerful framework and an excellent tool to help you diffuse the stress you may feel around money and replace some of your old thoughts that don't serve you with others that do.

In our $1,000 bank balance example, the fact (or circumstance or event) is that there's $1,000 in your bank account. This is neither good nor bad, enough or not enough, reassuring or stressful. It's just a number. The same thing is true for your student loan balance, your credit card statements, and your salary. They're just numbers. The negativity, anxiety, and stress you might feel comes from the story you tell yourself about those numbers.

When you find yourself feeling stressed, ask yourself what the facts are. Get very specific. "On December 18, 2021, at 11:00 a.m. EST, my checking account has a balance of $1,000." Here's how that might work in a coaching session.

DANA

Let's say Dana starts the session saying, "I'm so stressed out!"
"What are the facts?" I might ask.
"I'm broke!"
This isn't a fact. Even if Dana is, in fact, completely out of money (which is highly unlikely), "broke" is a value judgment or opinion. One person's "broke" is another person's Scrooge McDuck moment, so I suggest to Dana that "I'm broke" is a thought and ask her about the emotions that thought is bringing up in her.

"Anxiety!" she says. "I feel like my skin is a highway for electric ants. I'm prickly and panicky and tense. There's probably some shame in there too, but mostly it's just really scary. If I can't get my spending under control and pay off my consumer debt and my student loans, I'm going to end up homeless!"

Dana has gone from opening her credit card bill to thinking "I'm broke" to feeling anxious to catastrophizing. (Catastrophizing—worrying about events that haven't happened—is an action many people take in response to feeling anxious, one that creates a rather unpleasant feedback loop. Catastrophizing thoughts create more anxious feelings, which motivate more catastrophic thinking, which creates...You get the idea.)

Once Dana can focus on the actual facts—the dollar amount of her income and debts—her prefrontal cortex can finally kick in and start contributing something positive to the conversation. She might begin to talk to her anxiety from that logical place of planning and realize that even if her financial state is as dire as she thinks (and again, it almost never is), the very worst-case scenario she would actually face is having to move into her parents' basement. (Like "under a bridge," it's always the parents' basement, even if the parents still have the person's childhood bedroom exactly the way they left it.)

Moving back to your parents' house is not ideal. But it isn't the kind of life-threatening emergency Dana's primitive brain provided a response for. If Dana can realize this, she's much more likely to choose actions that are helpful rather than the one her brain went to automatically—catastrophizing (which often leads to avoidance or stress-shopping) and delivers exactly the kind of results that cause the unfavorable circumstance that triggered the thought-feeling-action cascade in the first place.

FROM THOUGHTS TO FEELINGS

Go back and look at the fact-finding exercise at the top of this chapter. With your new understanding, can you spot the difference between the ones that are actual facts (events or circumstances) and the ones that are thoughts you might have? Telling facts from thoughts is the critical first step in picking apart stress (or any other emotions) you may have about money.

With events and the thoughts about them separated, it's easier to see the connection between thoughts and the feelings they cause. This gives you the chance to pick different thoughts and feel different feelings. Here's what that looks like:

PRIYA

Priya came to see me because her divorce had, in her words, "ruined me financially." When we laid out the facts, it was apparent that the divorce had certainly altered her financial picture. She'd spent $50,000 on lawyers and had been ordered to pay her musician husband $200,000 in spousal support their first year apart. Even once she realized that it wasn't these numbers but her thoughts about them ("I'll never be able to catch back up"; "I'll have to sell the house"), she still felt powerless and defeated—like she had no control over her finances. She also believed she had no control over how she felt about the situation. "I've lost seventy-five percent of my wealth," she told me. "That's just a fact. How can I feel anything except helpless?"

I suggested she could feel angry, and she considered that. She could see the kind of thoughts that would lead from the same circumstances to a different emotion. If she thought about the injustice of having to pay spousal support to someone because he'd chosen to work in a less lucrative profession or, if she remembered his infidelity, she could get angry. Then she realized that if she thought about how unhappy she'd been in her marriage and how being single meant she could keep every cent she made the next year (and every year after that) for herself, she could start to feel excited about the future. It started to feel almost like the losses she'd incurred were a small price to pay for the kind of options she saw ahead.

We don't always have a lot of control over the circumstances in our lives, but we don't have to give them power over how we think and feel. No one and nothing can jump inside your body and force you to feel something.

> Most people think money—not having enough, working on getting more, managing what they have properly— is what's stressing them out. But it's not money (or the lack thereof) that causes stress; it's how you think about it.

A NEW DEFINITION OF STRESS

Women face a challenging cultural narrative about how we feel and manage emotions. Once we understand where they come from and what they're for, we have a great deal more choice about how we live and enjoy (or worry about) our lives and finances. Most people understandably believe that events cause emotions because so much of what goes into how we feel happens under the surface in the older, more primitive, and reactionary parts of our brain. It can be very difficult to separate our thoughts about an event from the facts of the event itself. Learning to tell the difference between circumstances (facts and events) and thoughts (emotion-creating opinions) can give us a deeper understanding and more choice about how we feel.

Money (or lack thereof) does not and cannot cause stress. Like every other emotion, stress is caused by thoughts that are simply words in your head and don't have to be believed. Understanding the circumstance-thought-feeling-action-result sequence gives us the tools we need to interrupt the way we feel by changing our thoughts so we cannot only think but feel differently about money.

TURNING INSIGHTS INTO ACTION

1. Refer back to the fact-finding exercise at the beginning of the chapter. Reexamine any statement you marked as a fact. What do you think now? (Hint: there are no facts on the list!)

2. Take five or ten minutes to write about a recent money situation from your life—perhaps checking your account balances or net worth or seeing your latest credit card or student loan statement.

   Write down all your thoughts. This is simply journaling—there is no right or wrong; there aren't even any answers. These are just your thoughts.

After you're done, circle only the facts. This is similar to the chapter exercise but flexing your new mindset this time. Tip: When it comes to money, facts are generally limited to actual numbers. Everything else is most likely a thought or interpretation of the numbers.

3. Choose a few thoughts from the above exercise. Are there other thoughts you could think about the situation? Who would you be and how would you feel with these new thoughts?

Old Myth: Money is stressful. If I had more, I'd feel better.

New Mindset: Money has no power over my emotions. How I feel is determined by what I think, and I'm the one in charge of my thoughts.

Even once you get good at separating events from thoughts and thoughts from feelings, there's a particular class of thoughts that deserve special attention—the judgments we all have about how we (and everyone else) earn, save, and spend. These special thoughts reflect our morals and deserve a chapter of their own.

CHAPTER 3

Myth: Money Is (Im)moral

Moral beliefs are some of the earliest we get from our parents and organized religion. They're often explicitly taught and vigorously enforced. What do you believe about the morality of money?

Right and Wrong

Mark each statement with a T if it's true, a B if it's a belief you hold, an S if it's a widely held belief you don't believe, or an F if it's false.

Stealing is wrong.

Giving to charity is good.

Easy money is unethical.

It's greedy or materialistic to want nice things.

Having money means you've sold out.

Wealth is proof you're living a good life and being rewarded.

Wealth is proof that you're living a corrupt life and being rewarded.

---

* * *

Everybody makes moral judgments all day long—about themselves and others. Many of those judgments feel true, but only circumstances can be "true." Moral judgments, like all thoughts and beliefs, have no face value. They cannot be true or false. It may be true for you that it's wrong to hunt people for sport (here's hoping!), but it's still "just" a judgment. Happily, it's a judgment many people share, which is why hunting people is illegal. In other words, it's truly criminal but not truly wrong. Legality is a circumstance; morality is an opinion.

Moral judgments are a special class of thought because their felt sense of trueness is so strong. Money is always a circumstance—a green piece of paper or a number on your screen—but it's a circumstance most people have lots of moral judgments about. Money, for better or worse, is so heavily freighted with moral judgments that we even make moral judgments about talking about it. This is why money is a taboo subject, meaning that even discussing it candidly can be socially risky.

I think one of the reasons many women struggle with feelings of guilt or shame around money is how few conversations we have about it. Most of us have talked to our female friends more and in greater detail about our sex lives than our finances. This lack of open discussion both comes from and reinforces our culture's moral judgments about money and about women and money.

Most people feel reluctant to talk about money. We've been taught it's impolite. It's a social rule for men and women, but men who brag about their income or what they just spent on a new car are usually seen as successful if arrogant. Women who do the same, however, are described with much tougher language.

In fact, many of our culture's unspoken moral rules are different or more extreme for women. It's somehow less crass for men to brag about wealth than it is for women. The term "good provider" is rarely applied to women, and "gold digger" rarely to men. Women have more trouble charging for their time, negotiating for higher salaries or lower prices, and celebrating their financial wins. We're also much more likely to apologize for our success or worry about being seen as doing something "just for the money."

WOMEN AND JUDGMENT

Not only are moral and social judgments harsher on women, but we also tend to be more sensitive to them. Whether it's tied to outdated social rules that put women in the place of needing to "catch" a good husband, or whether it goes back further to our hunter-gatherer, fight-or-flight, and tend-or-befriend origins (or even to "immoral" Eve), most women worry more than men do about what others think of them. The desire to be good, to people-please, and to avoid conflict is hardly unique to women, but we do seem to feel it more strongly. One outcome of this is that we may be more able to "see" the moral judgments of others.

Of course, all humans follow social norms to a greater or lesser degree, but for many women, the imperative to get the social norms right, to follow the rules, be "good," and excel against the clear benchmarks is driven by a desire for safety—because if we follow the rules, we'll be safe, right? But society doesn't reward us for it. There's no special Followed the Rules prize.

For many of us, this need to "get it right" feeds a perfectionism that shows up as striving—for better grades, thinner thighs, or greater public recognition, and it frequently comes with a focus on what's missing. In a way, perfectionists suffer from a kind of scarcity thinking with the "never enough" translating as "never good enough." Something could always be better. We may be making good money, but we feel like we're not making enough. Our grades or bodies or careers aren't good enough to meet our own demands because our standard is perfection, and we—despite our best efforts—are people.

Happily, these standards, like all other forms of judgment, are just thoughts, albeit ones that we may think below the surface of our conscious awareness. Like impulses from our primitive brain, these unconscious thoughts were added before we were old enough to audit them.

THIS IS YOUR BRAIN ON JUDGMENT

We're all born with our brain still in its original packaging and running its preloaded software, but we can download updates. Many of these new programs (ways of thinking) get added more-or-less automatically in the form of socialization and instructions from our parents, schools, and culture as we grow up. Because the part of our brain that can think critically about these updates (the prefrontal cortex) isn't fully developed until we're in our twenties, we download and run the new code without reading it first. In other words, by the time you leave your teens, you're running moral judgment programs in your brain, and you most likely didn't consciously choose any of them!

This doesn't mean that once it's fully online, your prefrontal cortex can override all of its original programming, but it can start to evaluate it. Your prefrontal cortex can think about what you think. It can recognize outdated or harmful programs and download a patch. As an adult, you can make choices about what to believe. This can feel like an empowering possibility and a frightening responsibility depending, in part, on your mindset.

THE SCARCITY MINDSET

Because our primitive brain's job is to keep us alive, it's programmed to constantly scan for danger. As we talked about, this means searching for (and often overreacting to) active threats in our environment, but it also watches for what isn't there—a lack of safety, food, or cover. Not having enough food was a serious threat to our survival once upon a time, as was not having enough allies on our side. Constantly looking for what's missing might have once helped us, but today it's a design flaw that keeps us from feeling okay with our lives as they are. Feeling safe was dangerous when our primitive brains first came online. Today, it robs us of well-deserved peace of mind.

REBECCA

Rebecca worked with me one-on-one over Zoom, and on our first call, she got straight to the point. She was an entrepreneur who'd gone into business for herself in 2010. When we met in 2020, she'd already doubled her business but didn't feel like she'd really arrived. "My company just isn't making enough," she told me. "I know I should be grateful for what I have—two kids, a good marriage, my own business—but I just feel like I've fallen short, and I definitely don't have enough income."

"What does that mean?" I asked her.

She thought about it for a moment. "I don't know. I have anxious thoughts about money, but I'm sitting here in my expensive office chair in an apartment with heat and electricity."

"So you have enough for today?"

"Yes, I guess so," she said. "It just isn't enough to make me feel like I've made it."

We talked a little about what she meant by "making it," and I explained the arrival fallacy to her. We'll talk more about it in Chapter 8, but briefly, as I told Rebecca, the arrival fallacy is a belief that our lives or careers have a destination. They're headed somewhere, and if we work hard enough and are good enough, we'll eventually get there. We will have arrived, and we'll feel complete. Even if we consciously know that life itself is the destination and that we don't really arrive until we die, the hidden belief can contribute to feelings of inadequacy or dissatisfaction. It combines with moral judgment ("I should be there by now"), perfectionism ("I've gotten somewhere, but it's not all there yet"), and scarcity thinking ("I'll never be enough to get there, and nowhere I get will ever be enough") to leave us feeling like we've failed for not doing what we know is impossible.

Rebecca could see the truth that she did, actually, have enough, but she didn't feel it, and it was keeping her from enjoying her successes and celebrating her wins. She needed a way to override her primitive brain's scarcity messaging, so I suggested she start an Enough Journal. Like the familiar Gratitude Journal, hers would provide a place where, at the end of each day, she could jot down three times in the past twenty-four hours where she had or was enough.

I told Rebecca that our brains are like heat-seeking missiles, with the heat they're searching for being the warm feeling of validation. Whatever judgments—recognized or hidden, moral or social—that we hold, our brains search out evidence that we're right. Rebeca's brain was constantly scanning for proof that her "not enough" belief was right and happily overlooking any to the contrary. Deliberately forcing herself to go looking for times when she had and was enough would disrupt that automatic pattern and start to retrain her brain.

Rebecca had never thought of herself as a perfectionist, but she could see the way that tendency was contributing to the trouble she was having feeling peaceful about her financial situation. "So I guess I am a perfectionist," she told me with a twinkle. "That thinking means I'm not perfect. I better fix it!"

THE MOTIVATIONAL TRIAD

To understand why moral judgments, social validation, and being right all feel so good, we need to learn a bit more about the way the primitive brain works. There are three distinct types of things that get its attention: things that are pleasurable, painful, or easy. These three drives—toward pleasure, away from pain, and along with what's easy—make up the brain's core programming.

The Motivational Triad

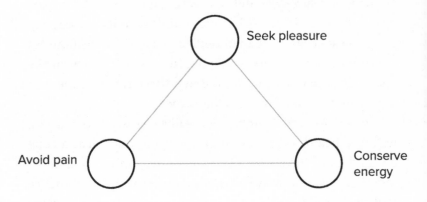

PLEASURE

When your primitive brain encounters something that promises pleasure, it will move toward it without giving much thought to downstream consequences or second-order effects. Our brains associate food and sex with pleasure since those are critical to our survival. Pleasure-seeking only gets us into trouble when we crave the dopamine hit at the expense of our well-being. High-calorie foods are an obvious example. Your brain takes pleasure in sugary or fatty foods and moves you in their direction because its code was written when such things were scarce, and our bodies were at an almost perpetual calorie deficit. Even when there was enough food in the moment, the future was uncertain, so we're motivated to stock up just in case. The idea that we might regret overeating at some later point doesn't even register. The primitive brain isn't convinced there'll be a later. Its "Don't die!" mandate is watching out for hungry tigers, not high triglycerides.

PAIN

The primitive brain's pain-avoidance programming is still useful. It's why you instinctively check the temperature before getting in the shower and put on boots when it's snowing. It's also why it's difficult to push yourself at the gym. If you start to feel breathless or achy, your brain gets increasingly insistent that you stop. Even when you know your lungs won't burst or your hamstrings snap, your primitive brain will get you to stop well before there's any actual danger because it doesn't like the discomfort. Your brain has the same relationship with emotional pain. It's almost as if it makes no difference to it whether it's your feet or your feelings your boss trampled on. Your brain is going to encourage you to avoid or be cautious around her next time either way.

EASE

In the first chapter, we talked about your brain's efficiency (or laziness), and this tendency shows up in the motivational triad as a preference for ease. This third leg of the triangle is more subtle than the drives toward pleasure and away from pain. When you consider doing something that will be difficult, your brain suggests something different. If the pain response is "Run for your life!" the response to difficulty is more like, "Hey, look over here. Wouldn't this easy thing be more fun?" It's almost as if your brain bounces off hard things. In addition, the brain also has a strong preference for the status quo. Not only is it usually easier to keep things the same than to go to the trouble of changing them, but your brain has solid evidence that things-as-they-are haven't killed you yet. There's no proof that a new way of thinking is equally survivable.

THE MOTIVATIONAL TRIAD AND MONEY

We've already described scenarios in which the motivational triad impacts your personal finances, but it's worth revisiting them now that we have the vocabulary. I'm sure you can see why "Money is complicated" is the first money myth we tackled. Your brain's tendency to shy away from things it thinks are difficult will make money something you're more likely to avoid. We talked about the role fear plays in our behavior in the previous "Money Is Stressful" chapter. This is the primitive brain firing up its "Danger! Danger!" response, which is what it does when it anticipates pain.

The motivational triad is operating within the "Money is (im)moral" myth too. Here, the relevant leg of the triangle is pleasure. It feels good to be right—it's a form of being certain. Being certain feels safe, and that makes our primitive brains very happy, even if the judgments we're accepting are unkind and confining.

COMMON JUDGMENTS

We've been happily breaking the taboo against talking about money for three chapters now, but here I want to dig a little deeper into some of the most common judgments people have about women and money: that we aren't good with it, shouldn't want it, can't negotiate effectively for it, and generally deserve less of it.

WOMEN AREN'T GOOD WITH MONEY

There are clear historical circumstances that surround this opinion. For years, women weren't allowed to own property or manage their own finances. Laws were made based on this arbitrary judgment, and those laws help keep the story alive. While laws have changed, there are still many people who carry this belief around. And we still live in a patriarchal culture—in most married couples, the man manages the finances. Many women have internalized this judgment. Most would reject it along gender lines, but many more women than men would agree with the statement, "I'm not good with money." This is neither true nor false. It's not a fact or circumstance. It's just an opinion, and opinions can change.

WOMEN SHOULDN'T WANT MONEY

Most people have opinions about the ways other people spend their money. Often, they're opinions that allow their holder to feel morally superior to others (which is pleasurable for the same reasons being right is). "I would never spend that much on shoes." "He doesn't give much to charity." They're also based on the idea that "frugality is virtuous, and greed is a sin" (one of the seven deadly kinds). The social bias against women appearing greedy is still strong enough that most of us have trouble charging what we're worth. It's also the reason for one of the stranger things I hear clients say: "It's not about the money."

I can't estimate the percentage of women entrepreneurs I've heard insist they're "not doing it for the money." Whether they've been in business for years or are just starting out, whether their company is successful or struggling, many women go out of their way to say that while the money is (or would be) great, it's not their main, and certainly not their only, motivation. I've never heard a man apologize for his ambition this way. Men seem to have no trouble admitting that the money is the point. Passion or service is (or would be) great, but they're in business to make money.

I want women to flip this script! I firmly believe that if we truly want to be of service, the best thing we can do is get rich.

I believe a world of wealthy and powerful women would be a better world. I believe that as more women make more, we'll raise up other women. We'll contribute more to our communities and do more to ensure equality. We will support families, improve childcare and education, care for our planet, and increase engagement. I'm not saying women should get rich to give more away. I'm saying the greater the percentage of wealth in the hands of women, the better the world will be. (As a point of interest, we currently hold about 32 percent of the world's wealth.)

WOMEN ARE INFERIOR NEGOTIATORS

This judgment is the end product of several stacked judgments beginning with something like "Women aren't as tough as men." It's true that, on average, women are more conflict-averse than men. This may be because we've never been likely to fare well in physical confrontations. While most educated professional women today don't need to worry about their physical safety, we have thousands of years of history behind us in which that wasn't the case. (Although, weirdly, it's still legal for a man to beat his wife in Arkansas as long as he doesn't do it twice in a month.) People who accept this opinion as fact, when confronted with a tough woman, make negative judgments about her. A tone of voice that is "commanding" in a man is "bitchy" in a woman. Behaviors that are seen as showing leadership in men are labeled "bossiness" in women.

Women, sensitive to this, have a choice: be judged negatively or negotiate less aggressively. Men, if offered the same choice, might make the same decision. But they aren't. (Even the word "aggressive" has a different connotation applied to men and women.) Women typically negotiate for themselves less effectively than men, not because they are women, but because they're held to a different set of social rules and have been socialized to care more about others' opinion of them than their own.

WOMEN ARE WORTH LESS

While very few people would put it this bluntly, it's what the facts of our economy say. Money is a measure of value, and women have less of it in general and make less per hour (with the gender–pay gap even greater for women of color). The burden of raising children falls disproportionately on us. We're much more likely than men to leave the workforce or compromise our professional lives when our children are small, which leaves us at a disadvantage later in our careers. We're also more likely than men to take on the additional work later of caring for our aging parents. In fact, depending on a daughter in your old age is the traditional rule in many cultures.

WOMEN ARE GOLD DIGGERS

While I don't know many people who still actually hold this judgment, its legacy is visible in our cultural squeamishness about prenups. Marriage is—and always has been—a contract. Statistically, the chance that a marriage will end in divorce (even for a smart, educated, type-A woman) is greater than zero. Even if only every fourth marriage ended before death did them part, one-in-four odds aren't so small you'd ignore them if you had the same chance of dying in a bicycle accident. (The odds there are only about 1:3,825, and I bet you wear your helmet anyway!)

If you're getting legally married, you're entering into a legally binding agreement. It can be the boilerplate agreement with its "what to do if it ends" strategy laid out by the divorce laws of your state, or you can write it together for your specific circumstances. People write their own vows and get their wedding clothes tailored; shouldn't the actual marriage contract be equally fitted to you?

But I get it. It's a hard topic to raise. Talking about money is uncomfortable. It's also one of the top sources of conflict in a marriage, so maybe some practice discussing it before the wedding is a good idea. As we'll discuss in the next chapter, the ability to have hard conversations is the currency of your dreams. Also, if you think talking with your partner about how to divide your combined assets is uncomfortable now when you hold each other in such high regard, think about how much worse it would be to need to talk about it for the first time as the marriage was ending, when your opinions of each other are likely to be coming from something other than the best part of yourselves.

CHALLENGING JUDGMENTS

These all-to-common judgments are relatively easy to reject, and most of the women I know and work with already have, even if they may still feel the pressure of some. But there are other, subtler "automatic updates" we download directly from our parents and culture and run through our heads. These moral judgment programs run deep and feel true. Our primitive brain's motivational triad (which seeks out validation, acceptance, and certainty) makes our moral judgments difficult to question and replace. We can still download new programming and reject our culture's judgments about women and money.

We can also challenge our own. Look again at the list I gave you at the beginning of this chapter. Can you recognize now that none of them are true? Look particularly closely at the ones you marked with a T and a B. I'm not saying you have to stop believing them. Beliefs are useful and important. What I am saying, however, is that they have no face value. Money isn't good or bad, moral or immoral. Money is like a hammer. It can hammer a nail or your thumb with outcomes you like and don't like, but the hammer isn't bad when it hurts you.

Money is value neutral.

A NEW DEFINITION OF MORALITY IN MONEY

Money is the subject of many different kinds of thinking, but the moral judgments we make about it are some of the hardest to recognize as "just thoughts," in part because there's a taboo against talking about money.

TURNING INSIGHTS INTO ACTION

1. Refer back to the exercise at the beginning of the chapter. What do you think now?
2. Were you taught that the pursuit of money was bad or greedy?
3. What were you taught about "rich people"?
4. If you overheard someone talking about you, and they said, "She's rich," what would be your immediate response? Is it a positive or negative response? Why?
5. What were you taught about "poor people"?
6. Do you feel guilty about spending money on yourself? Why or why not?

Old Myth: Money is (im)moral. Having (or not having) it can make me a bad person or prove I'm a good one.

New Mindset: Money is a tool and no more innately "good" or "evil" than a hammer.

Of course, even if we were able to recognize all our moral judgments about money as the opinions they are, we'd probably still have plenty of "shoulds" and "shouldn'ts" left related to purely practical questions. If you've occasionally felt guilt for how you've spent money or wondered why you can't seem to bring your spending under control, you may think you don't have enough willpower. In the next chapter, I'll explain why nobody does and why it doesn't help anyway.

CHAPTER 4

Myth: Willpower Works

Rather than another quiz, we'll start this chapter with a thought experiment:

Imagine

Imagine you're walking down a leafy quasi-suburban street. Maybe you're meeting a friend for lunch at a café. You left home a little early because you wanted to stop into that cute woman-owned bookstore nearby and because parking would be easier. Somewhere between your car and the café, you're stopped dead in your tracks by the perfect handbag. You've been looking for something like this—sleek but roomy, over the shoulder but not cross-body, leather with just the right amount of brass.

Try to put yourself in this moment, the feeling of delighted surprise, the curiosity, the longing. If bags don't speak to you, substitute what does—shoes, jewelry, designer dresses—but find the feeling.

You want that thing. But you recognize the brand. It may be perfect, but it's going to be expensive.

You want it, but should you buy it?

You really, really want it.

Let's say you dash into the boutique (hey, it's locally owned, so at least that's good, right?), and you buy the bag. You love it! You arrive at lunch only a few minutes late, but your friend totally understands when you show her the bag.

On the way back to the car and the next two times you go out with the bag on your shoulder, it feels great. Then the credit card bill comes, and you look at your new bag sitting there beside your old bag close to the closet, where there are at least another six bags. The guilt gets you. You shouldn't have done that. You feel terrible. You should have been more disciplined. You call yourself some unkind names and tell yourself to face facts—you have a spending problem.

* * *

You don't have a spending problem. You spend money perfectly well and in accordance with your plans and values most of the time. The problem is over-spending. I know this sounds like a moral judgment, but it isn't. I'm using "over" here the way a glass of water can be overfull. The difference between spending and over-spending (as between any indulgence and over-indulgence) is one of degree and outcome.

OVER-SPENDING

Spending $500 on a handbag can mean a well-earned reward or blowing the month's rent. Being a little overextended because of a shopping spree isn't the same as owing more on your credit card than you make in a year. It's a difference, not of dollar amount, but of net outcome. To use a food example, a cookie or two can be a nice treat, but a box or two isn't good for anyone, and the consequences range from spending an extra hour on the treadmill to dying young.

Almost everyone over-somethings sometimes, and almost all women who do carry a certain amount of shame around it. We may be reluctant to talk about it because we're embarrassed. It can feel like admitting you have a problem. We think our over-spending is a moral failing or indicates we lack discipline. Particularly as successful, professional women, we feel like we should be in better control. But you can put your shame away. There's nothing wrong with you. You (like every other human being) are wired to overindulge. This isn't about being impulsive or lacking self-control; it's about having more desire than you can manage. Over-spending is really overdesiring.

THIS IS YOUR BRAIN ON DESIRE

When I introduced the motivational triad in the last chapter, I explained that the primitive brain is motivated by pleasure.

It likes pleasure and wants more, and it lets you know this by throwing feelings like desire, hunger, lust, and craving at you. Most of the time, your primitive brain and your prefrontal cortex agree on what to do about the situation, and you buy the umbrella you want or eat the sandwich you're hungry for. But not always.

PLEASURE AND DESIRE

Remember, our primitive brains have only one big idea—Don't die! On the motivational triad of pain, pleasure, and ease, the pain leg uses fear to move us away from things that might kill us. Pleasure uses desire to move us toward the things that keep us alive. At least that's what the primitive brain thinks it's doing. It doesn't understand time and has no conception of downstream costs. And again, most of the time, this arrangement works well. The prefrontal cortex helps get the primitive brain's reasonable desires met and doesn't act on the ones that it knows aren't good for us. Most of the time.

If you doubt the power of your prefrontal cortex, put yourself back in the shopping story. There you are, looking in the window, wanting. If you go inside, check the price tag, and see the bag costs $3 million, what happens? My bet is you'd walk out pretty easily. But to understand how a desire gets strong enough to override your prefrontal cortex's reasonable restraints, we need to go a little deeper into how your brain works.

Your primitive brain likes pleasure and creates a desire to alert us to things it believes will feel good. It bases that belief on both its preloaded programming and on experience. In the handbag example, you bought the bag—you loved it, your friend loved it—and you felt great.

On a biological level, "feeling great" translates into "large release of dopamine." Your primitive brain pays close attention to things that cause such large releases of dopamine and keeps an eye out for them.

When an experience delivers mild pleasure, our brain releases a bit of dopamine. When an experience delivers a very concentrated dose of pleasure, our brains pour on the dopamine to make sure we're really paying attention. Dopamine teaches us what to seek out more of to feel more pleasure. In other words, dopamine teaches us desire. If an apple delivers a small, happy experience of sweetness, but a candied apple delivers more, the next time we see an apple, we might feel a small amount of desire, but the candied apple will trigger a much larger dose of desire because, in the past, it delivered a larger dose of pleasure.

You can buy quite a lot of candied apples before you get into over-spending territory, so let's use the candy-apple-red bottoms of a $600 pair of shoes for our example here. If your brain has marked shoe shopping with dopamine, a beautiful pair of Louboutins will cause desire. Whether that desire is overdesire has nothing to do with the shoes, their price tag, or the dopamine your brain will supply when you buy them. If you can easily afford them or are rewarding yourself with them, or if you have a special occasion coming up that justifies them, your desire for them is not excessive. Only if they will later cause you pain (emotional pain, not foot pain) is your desire for them excessive.

To go back to our thought experiment, if you've bought a new handbag a few times and each time, it's caused a major release of dopamine, the next time you pass a new one on the way to lunch, your primitive brain will pull you up short. If it's come to associate buying bags with floods of dopamine, it will then crank desire up to eleven.

If you buy the bag and get the dopamine rush, it reinforces the association and the desire. The primitive brain is primitive. It doesn't associate the subsequent feelings of guilt and regret with the bag—the credit card bill is too far separated in time. Instead, it associates the bill itself with pain and sends fear messages to you when you open the mail.

> This inability to correctly line up cause and effect across time is the reason why the true pleasure of a lean and healthy body doesn't always win out over the false pleasure of French fries and cheesecake, and why the true pain of a hangover isn't reliably enough to make the false pleasure of that third drink undesirable. For readers of this book, a few extra pounds and the occasional rough morning are probably as far as the damage done by false pleasures goes, but their pursuit can ruin lives.

But what happens if you don't buy the bag—if the desire isn't satisfied? Most people lump desire and pleasure together, so it can be difficult to realize that while pleasure feels great, desire is actually pretty uncomfortable. The feeling of desire and especially of overdesire is designed to make us take action. Not taking action can be an intensely unpleasant feeling.

UNCOMFORTABLE FEELINGS

"Negative" emotions are, by definition, ones that feel bad, and the instinct to avoid feeling them is more or less baked into us and completely understandable. If physical pain didn't motivate us to avoid physically painful situations, we'd be in trouble! But our brains can't tell the difference between physical and emotional pain.

In Chapter 2, I mentioned that feelings are the fuel for everything we do, and that's true, but the truth is that most people don't actually enjoy having strong feelings. Even very intense good feelings can make us uncomfortable just by their sheer intensity. There's a cultural bias against emotion in favor of reason, which comes from an outdated model of human nature and which historically designates women as weaker, more emotional, and less rational than (and therefore inferior to) men. All of which is ridiculous.

There's no reason to believe women are inherently more emotional, although men may be subject to more intense socialization around showing their emotions and certainly the "male" emotional behaviors of shouting and intimidation are more acceptable than the "feminine" ones of crying or comforting. But all of us have been taught that a loss of emotional control is bad, and most of us, therefore, get uncomfortable feeling much of anything very strongly. As a result, we've developed four ways of handling our feelings: we can resist them, react to them, allow them, or try to avoid them in the first place.

Buffering

"Buffering" is a term for using external things to change (buffer) how we feel. It describes things we do to hide from reality and avoid feeling negative emotions, behaviors that keep us from fully experiencing our lives and provide only temporary relief from the emotion we're trying to avoid. Often, this equates to avoiding the kind of situations that your prefrontal cortex knows your primitive brain associates with high-dopamine-creating situations but that it knows come with negative downstream consequences. In our shopping example, you'd change your lunch spot or start carrying cash for your meal and leaving your credit card at home to create a buffer between yourself and the exciting/ dangerous store.

Resisting

Resisting an emotion means white-knuckling your way through it or waiting for it to go away by tightening up. In our purse-buying example, it's standing outside the shop window, staring at the bag, wanting it, and not going inside despite the tension building inside you. And it does build. Resisting desire increases desire. Your poor, dumb primitive brain thinks surely, you're just not hearing its request for the thing that gives it the dopamine you both enjoy, and it gets louder.

What you resist persists.

Your primitive brain is capable of increasing desire to a truly unbearable level. This is why you need to have some compassion for yourself when you're at home looking at the other bags and the credit card bill. You aren't a weak person. Your desire is just very, very strong. If you're counting on willpower to resist overdesire, you're working against your basic biology.

Reacting

When you react to an emotion, you respond to it by "giving into" whatever the feeling is prompting you to do. It's what happened in the first version of the story—you reacted to your desire for the handbag by buying it. Reacting closes the desire loop by satisfying it and reinforces it because, clearly, it works!

Allowing

Allowing is emotional judo. It sees the desire but neither resists nor reacts. You shift your mind's eye from the bag to the desire for the bag. You feel your feelings. This is uncomfortable. Your primitive brain gets very upset when you don't react the way it wants you to, no matter how loudly it shouts. It leaves the desire wheel and runs over to the danger button. This is something new. New is dangerous. It's a lion!

Your prefrontal cortex knows there's no lion. It knows what you're feeling won't kill you. It can just let the primitive brain do its thing, feel the feelings it kicks up and allow them. It's a little like an adult coolly watching a child wear themself out throwing a tantrum. But it isn't easy, and very few of us have been taught how.

Most educated, professional women spend most of our time in our heads rather than in our bodies feeling our feelings, and we really struggle with this. Our tendency is to try thinking our way out of feeling or talking to ourselves about why we shouldn't be feeling what we are.

We need to relearn how to feel.

Because the feeling persists when we try to resist it, we often think we're feeling a feeling because we're resisting it, but resistance creates tension. Allowing creates relief. It's a bit like the difference between trying not to breathe and breathing. We've been breathing in constricted gasps for so long that we need to learn and practice allowing our feelings to simply move through us. It's a skill like any other, and I'll talk you through it later in this chapter. It takes time to develop, but it's worth it. It's one of the most important abilities you can train yourself in. Once you master it, you can radically change your relationship with yourself, with others, and with money.

The Power of Allowing

Brooke Castillo, founder of the Life Coach School and author of It Was Always Meant to Happen That Way, calls discomfort the "currency of your dreams." Tim Ferris, the author of The 4-Hour Workweek, says that "a person's success in life can usually be measured by the number of uncomfortable conversations he or she is willing to have." The ability to neither resist nor react to uncomfortable feelings really is a superpower.

Brave people aren't fearless; they're just able to allow their fear to be there in the room while they do what they need to do. Entrepreneurs aren't exceptionally innovative; they're just able to allow their anxiety to do its thing while they consistently place bet after bet on themselves. Most public speakers aren't natural performers; they're just able to allow their jitters to be there when they walk out onstage. The ability to allow uncomfortable feelings is also the engine behind the ability to unlearn overdesire.

UNLEARNING OVERDESIRE

When I tell people it's possible to unlearn desire, they rarely believe me straightaway. It seems like a crazy idea, I know. But you've already unlearned many desires. Do you still pine for that boy you had your first crush on? Do you still want anything you once urgently begged Santa for? What you desire isn't who you are. It changes. You leave some behind and acquire new ones. If you learned how to desire handbags, you can unlearn it.

Unlearning overdesire requires putting together ideas from a few of our previous chapters. In "Money Is Complicated," we learned that we don't have to believe what we think. When your brain thinks it needs a new handbag or thinks the handbag you've just seen is the perfect one, you don't have to believe it.

In Chapter 2, we traced the path from event to thought to feeling to action to result. Typically, the event of seeing something desirable causes the thought "I want that," which causes the action "buy that," which causes the result "having that." Having gotten something you wanted feels, at least momentarily, good. In Chapter 3, we talked about the motivational triad, which we've already seen at work in the handbag example. An "I want that" thought triggers overdesire because the pleasure piece of the triad has learned that buying bags pays off big in dopamine. (It's these big payoffs in dopamine that cause overdesire. This is why nobody gets addicted to water.)

Unlearning desire means proving that part of the triad wrong. When it no longer believes buying bags will give it pleasure, it will stop wanting to buy bags. Unfortunately, there's only one way to teach it this lesson—to stop buying bags. To stop buying bags before you stop wanting them, you have to learn a different response to desire. There are only four options: buffering, resisting, reacting, and allowing.

Reacting is no longer really an option. (No matter what you may try to tell yourself about "one last" or "a fresh start," buying bags to stop buying bags won't fly.) That leaves three other options. You can, of course, keep trying to buffer or resist, but if you have an overdesire problem, you have proof that neither works very well.

To unlearn overdesire, you have to allow it.

Not buying the bag and allowing your overdesire to just be there will (eventually) decouple seeing pretty bags from strong doses of pleasure until your primitive brain finally lumps them in with other pleasures you outgrew. You no longer crave them any more than you still want Barbies. To see how this works, let's rewind the tape to the place when you stopped suddenly on your way to lunch.

THE BAG IN THE WINDOW, TAKE TWO

There you are on the leafy street looking forward to seeing your friend but with plenty of time. You're walking along happily looking in windows, enjoying the exercise, when there it is. The perfect bag—slender but spacious, beautiful leather. You can see immediately what it would look like on you. How useful it would be. You want it. You really, really want it.

So you notice the wanting. You observe it. It doesn't feel good. You want it to go away, and all you need to do to make it stop is walk in there and buy the bag. It wouldn't hurt to just try it on, right?

But your prefrontal cortex has made a commitment to teaching your primitive brain to stop overdesiring handbags. You could just walk away. But you don't. You remind yourself: feelings are for feeling. So you simply feel the overdesire—the deep discomfort of it—and describe it to yourself without judgment as if you were trying to explain it to an alien who's never felt desire. Where in your body do you feel it most keenly? Is it a tightness in your chest? An itch or crawling between your shoulder blades? A feeling of heat or chill in your stomach or your hands? You observe it. You tell yourself: what I'm feeling are sensations in my body caused by a thought in my head.

That's all it is. You can handle that, right?

It isn't easy, and it doesn't feel great. As you stand there, the feeling intensifies. Then it starts to fade. All feelings are temporary. Your primitive brain can't keep banging the alarm bell for long.

And now it's had a new experience. You can feel that feeling and not die. The desire ebbs away, and you get to the café a little late and not as giddy as you were when you had a new bag, but calmer and proud of yourself. You did what you intended to do. You're just that little bit more in control of your life.

Your financial freedom is worth the
discomfort of unlearning overdesire.

PRACTICE

Here's a low-stakes way to experiment with how it feels to simply allow uncomfortable feelings. The next time you hear your cellphone's text message alert, don't look at your phone. Wait. Can you hear your thoughts? "Who is that? What do they want? Has something happened? Is something wrong?" What are you feeling? Name your feelings to yourself. Describe them. Observe them. Allow them. Feel your feelings.

What happens? Did you feel the intensity of your feelings crest and then fade? Did you introduce a buffer by distracting yourself or walking away? Did you pick up your phone? Did you feel your desire to look at your phone but resist it, tensing up against the desire and clenching yourself against it?

You can't fail this experiment. Whichever one or combination of the four ways of dealing with a feeling you employ, simple awareness and observation are all you need for success.

Willpower doesn't work. Allow power does.

A NEW DEFINITION OF WILLPOWER

Over-spending, which we've defined as spending with a net negative outcome, results from overdesire, and willpower—trying to resist intense desire by sheer strength of will—doesn't work. This isn't because you're weak. It's because you're biologically programmed to actively go after things that have delivered large hits of dopamine in the past. But you're not powerless in the face of your programming. You can unlearn desire by allowing your uncomfortable feelings of overdesire without buffering, resisting, or acting on them.

TURNING INSIGHTS INTO ACTION

Feeling a feeling is also called *processing* a feeling. This just means you feel the feeling in your body *all the way through* without resisting, avoiding, or reacting to it until it goes away. You simply allow all the physical sensations of the emotion to percolate and dissipate without letting yourself (your brain) interrupt it.

Young children (particularly toddlers) provide a beautiful example of emotion processing. They do it naturally. They *feel* their feelings. Fiercely. Then they get on with life.

HOW TO **FEEL** A FEELING

1. Stop thinking. (Yes, I can hear you: "Sure, that's easy. There's an off button around here somewhere.")
2. Close your eyes and bring your awareness to your body.
3. Take a deep breath. Take a few more.

4. Do a body scan.
   a. Focus your awareness and attention on your body. Scan it from head to toe and locate where you are *feeling* sensations—emotional or physical. Your goal is only to develop more awareness of feeling sensations regardless of where they originate in your body.
   b. Describe what you are feeling physically. (Example: "My jaw is heavy and tingly. I feel a heaviness in my chest.")
   c. Asking yourself these questions may help: "What am I feeling now? Where am I feeling this in my body? What color is this feeling? Is this a big or small feeling? Is it soft or hard? Is it fast or slow? Is it moving? How does this feeling make me want to react?"
   d. As you do the scan, check in with yourself. Remind yourself that you are simply feeling sensations. You are safe. The sensations you feel are temporary.
   e. If you can easily recognize what you are feeling (anxious, happy etc.), ask yourself, "How do I know I am feeling ____ (anxious, happy, etc.)?"
   f. Describe the sensations you feel that constitute that feeling.

When you first do this, your mind will wander and may urge you to stop and do something else. This is normal.

You may find that it's easier to feel some feelings than others. Some feelings are "loud"—with stronger sensations in the body. Others are more subtle. Joy, for example, is a "quiet" feeling. Anxiety and anger are "louder" feelings. This is normal too.

SUGGESTED PRACTICES

1. Feeling Practice

Practice feeling your feelings twice a day. Set an alarm. When it goes off, simply ask yourself: "What am I feeling now? How do I know I am feeling ___? Where am I feeling it? How do I want to react to this feeling and why?"

2. Top Three

Before bed, think back over the day and identify your top three feelings. (You'll likely find these are your top three feelings overall.) Ask yourself: "Why do I think I have these same top three feelings? How would my life change if my top three feelings changed? Would I like any or all of them to be different? If not, why not? If so, which ones and what would I rather feel instead?"

3. Worst One

What is the worst feeling you can imagine having to face? What would it feel like in your body? Describe it in detail. Where in your body would you feel it, and how would it feel?

Have you gone to great lengths to avoid feeling this feeling? Why?

Remember, a feeling is a temporary sensation in the body. It is harmless. If you were willing to feel this feeling without fear, how might you act differently? What would you do? Why?

Old Myth: Willpower works. I just need to be stronger and resist over-spending more diligently.

New Mindset: I can have compassion for myself and simply allow my strong feelings and feel them—without acting on them. Eventually, this will teach my primitive brain to stop overdesiring things that have a net negative outcome.

It can be very liberating to realize you can unlearn desires that have a net negative impact on your life. Even before you start acting from your new mindset, let yourself take in enough to stop saying negative things to yourself about how you spend money. Then, let's talk about how you can get more of it!

CHAPTER 5

Myth: Everybody Works for Money

By now, I imagine you're getting suspicious of my inventory and quizzes. Several times now, I've asked you to delineate between things on a list only to go back and tell you there were actually no distinctions there. Still, before we begin this chapter on making money and income, I have a few questions for you to answer. And this time, I promise, there are no wrong answers.

Question and Answer

How much money do you want to make? Take a moment and think about it. If you've made it this far into a book about money, you're clearly interested in change. If I asked you, right now, to set a goal for how much money you wanted to make, what number would you write down? Take a moment. Think about it. "I want to earn (number) dollars." Do you have a number? Excellent.

Now think about your thinking. How did you come up with your number? Assuming you didn't just write this exercise off as ridiculous, when you started calculating, what factors did you take into account? Did you balance your dream income against your other commitments or pleasures? Did you consider the type of work you do, the time involved, and the typical earnings within your profession?

* * *

I'm not going to try and guess your number because that's not the way books work. I am going to make a prediction based on my experience with asking this question to thousands of women. I predict you're making two assumptions that you don't know you're making, and that there are beliefs you have without necessarily knowing you have them, which factored into selecting your number.

If you chose a number that doesn't at least triple what you're making now, I predict that you thought something like, "I don't want to make the kind of sacrifices it takes to earn more." Beneath this thought is the assumption that there's some kind of zero-sum time-money relationship at work that requires you to have less of something to have more money. When you thought about how much you wanted to make, where did you imagine the money coming from? My guess is the only source of income you considered (barring inheritance or the lottery) is your salary.

These two unrecognized ideas—that earning more requires sacrifices and that getting a salary is the only way to earn an income—just kept you from imagining any number you could have chosen. I put no restrictions on the question. I didn't say, "How much do you want to make a year" or "How much do you think you can make." Any limits you put on that number came from your beliefs about where money comes from and how it's acquired.

YOUR INCOME CEILING

Beyond these two hidden assumptions, many women seem to have other kinds of resistance to filling in the "I want to make $___" blank with a big number. Try it for yourself. What number can you put in that empty space and finish the sentence with conviction? Do you hit a ceiling on what you're comfortable desiring?

Not all women have this unacknowledged ceiling, but I've never met a man who does. Our cultural bias against "greedy" women or even ambitious ones can manifest here, holding us back. Sometimes questions of worthiness show up too. I've worked with many women who've started to cry, realizing there's a threshold number they can't really imagine exceeding. "I don't feel like I deserve more than that" is typically the way they express it.

Sometimes, women have an unacknowledged ceiling that's a bit under what their husbands make. They begin to feel anxious when they experiment with the idea of making significantly more than their spouse.

Often, the myth that money is immoral contributes too. On some level, many people believe that they would sacrifice some of their morality if they made more than a set number. Sometimes, when they dig down into their thinking, they realize they believe they'd have to do unethical things to make more than their chosen number. More often, there's an unrealized fear that if they made more than a certain unarticulated amount, the money would corrupt them. I've even heard people say, "There's no way anyone who makes more than a million a year can be a good person." It's as though money itself would exert some negative moral force on them.

I've worked with several women who, without really realizing it, had set an income ceiling for themselves of $500,000 a year. I'm not sure why that number recurs, but it does. Beyond that, it starts to feel unreal or impossible—like any version of you making more than that would be fundamentally un-you-like. For some people, their identity starts to feel a bit unstable at a much lower threshold.

It's worth spending some time considering whether you have an income ceiling because I can almost guarantee you'll never exceed it. As we learned in Chapter 2, thoughts create feelings that drive actions, and what you do determines what you get in life. If your thinking is literally restricting what you can imagine making, how much do you think investing in changing that thinking might be worth?

WHAT MONEY IS

Most people think money comes from some combination of time and effort, but all money is, according to Webster's, is "something generally accepted as a medium of exchange, a measure of value, or a means of payment." In other words, money measures value.

Before the Industrial Revolution, we used money to buy shoes from the cobbler and meat from the butcher. Although the craftsperson's time was part of the equation, it wasn't until shoe factories needed assembly line workers that people started being paid by the hour. Cobblers could make shoes whenever the light or the mood was right. Factories require more predictability in their workers, which is where the idea of a Monday to Friday, nine-to-five work week originated. We'll talk more about how the Industrial Revolution changed our relationship with time in Chapter 8, but to understand income, it's important to understand that the hourly wage—and its logical extension, the yearly salary—are arbitrary and recent ideas. They're also incredibly limiting. None of us have more than twenty-four hours in a day, and if your time is your only source of income, then every hour you spend not working lowers what you earn.

It's a very transactional way of looking at work, money, and time. An hourly (or yearly) rate of pay is functionally an employer telling an employee what that person's time is worth to them. It motivates people to do the minimum rather than their best. If you're getting $20 an hour whether you run or ramble, why spend more energy than necessary? It also motivates employers to treat people like work dispensers and employees to keep their hands out, expecting additional money for any modicum of additional work. Finally, it makes employees entirely dependent on their jobs for all of their income. This, in turn, puts your employer in a position of power over you and contributes to the anxiety-inducing thoughts about what would happen if you lost your job.

Money is a way of assigning value to something, but value is extremely subjective. This is why there are people who are willing to pay more for luxury cars or jewelry than you think they're worth and why someone will pay for the shoes you no longer value and give to Goodwill. How much something is worth is determined by what someone else is willing to pay for it. This means it's the buyer, not the seller, who determines value.

Likewise, no matter how much you think you're worth or how valuable you believe your contribution is, no matter how hard you work or how much education you have (or how much it cost), your salary will be determined by how much someone is willing to pay you for your value, and you'll be dependent on your job to give you money. Luckily, your time, expertise, and effort aren't the only thing you have of value.

WHERE VALUE COMES FROM

By now, it's old news to you that thoughts create results. They can also create money—and not in the "think it, and it will manifest" way. Every new invention or technology in the world was first an idea (a thought) in someone's mind. Apple is a multibillion-dollar company not because Steve Jobs worked billions of hours but because he had billion-dollar ideas. I'm not suggesting you need to think up the next iPhone, but you're entirely capable of creating ideas that are worth more than you're getting hourly or annually. You can create value from your ideas. Of course, nobody paid Steve Jobs for his ideas until he'd executed on at least the first few. But have no doubt that you can create value by thinking of ideas that are valuable. (More on this in the next section!)

RESULTS

When people buy an iPhone, they're not paying for the actual phone—a little silver rectangle—they're paying for the things it allows them to do. They're paying for the ability to listen to music, make a call, take a photo, deposit a check, and all the other functions their phone provides. Likewise, when you buy medicine, you're not paying for how long it takes the pharmacist to put the pills in the bottle. You're paying for the destruction of the bacteria that's causing your sinus infection. My private coaching clients don't pay for their weekly hour on Zoom, but for the result that hour produces in their lives.

Some more progressive companies are beginning to consider their salaried workers as being paid for results. The rise of at-home working during the pandemic may have encouraged both companies and workers to focus less on hours-at-your-desk and more on work accomplished.

When value comes from the results being delivered, its price depends on how badly someone needs the result and how hard those results are to come by. If you have an idea that can deliver results that few others can and that many want, you've found a source of value that has nothing to do with the time it takes you.

EXPERTISE

Closely related to creating value by delivering results is the value of your expertise. When I was a practicing physician, people would occasionally complain that they'd seen their doctor for just five minutes and been billed hundreds of dollars. They didn't realize that what they were really paying for was the ten years it took the doctors to acquire the knowledge and experience that enabled her to make an accurate diagnosis in "just five minutes."

THE ONE RULE OF WEALTH

We were trained to believe that our only access to money was to be paid for our time working for companies that created value, but we are capable of creating value directly in the world ourselves. This is where real wealth comes from. Rich people (who didn't inherit their wealth) created it by adding value not to a company owned by an employer but to what they owned themselves. In other words, if you want to be wealthy, solely working for someone else isn't going to get you there. What will? Acquiring and growing assets.

The one rule of wealth: acquire and grow assets.

WHAT ASSETS ARE

People often think that investing in assets is something only rich people can do, but that's not the case. An asset is simply something you own that puts money in your pocket: a retirement account that accrues interest, real estate you own that pays rent, intellectual property that pays royalties or brings in passive income, a company you own (if it brings in money), and any stocks that pay dividends.

It's not at all unusual for successful, professional people to discover they have very few assets—often only one or two: a retirement account and perhaps some shares in the company they work for. Considering that the dominant cultural formula for wealth is "Go to school, get a good job, and work hard," this isn't surprising. But it isn't going to make you rich. Only getting and growing assets will do that. Still, people think of investing in assets as something they'll start doing once they have more money or after they've paid off their student loans. It's what they'll do with the "extra" money (whatever that is).

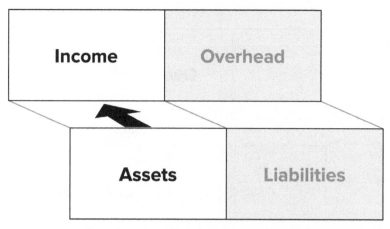

Assets put money in your pocket, AKA income.

SOME THINGS THAT AREN'T ASSETS

Your home is not an asset. Although you may have some equity in it, not only is it not putting money into your pocket, but it's actively taking it out. Jewelry is not an asset. No matter how much yours may be worth, if you're not renting it out or finding some other way for it to make money for you every month, it's not an asset. Neither are boats, cars, or art.

THIS IS YOUR BRAIN ON ASSETS

If you're realizing you have very few assets, don't worry! There's a solid, biologically based reason for not already having more: Your brain doesn't like investing. To your primitive brain with its motivational triad, investing looks almost designed to fail. It's not easy. There's a risk of pain (losing money), and any pleasure that it might yield is so removed

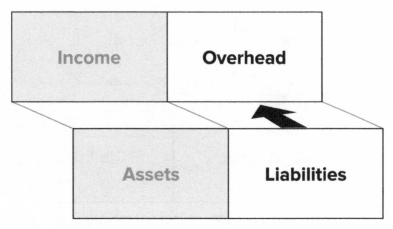

Liabilities take money in your pocket, AKA overhead.

in time that it's irrelevant. In contrast, while not as easy and pleasurable as shopping, paying off debt looks very appealing.

Paying off debt is easy. It's rewarding to watch the totals dwindle, and our culture heaps paying off debt with praise. We'll talk more about how to think about debt in the next chapter. Here, it's just a point of contrast. Paying off debt won't put money in your pocket. Still, people often use it as an excuse not to start buying and growing assets. I want you to recognize it as the clever avoidance tactic of your motivational triad-driven brain.

If you've gotten this far in the book—much less made it through school to be successful in a professional career—you already have enough prefrontal cortex control to override your primitives brain's aversion to investing, so let's take its objections one at a time:

Pain: Your brain foresees the possibility of the emotional pain of "failure" if any of your assets end up losing money.

- Ease: Your primitive brain doesn't like new things, and learning how to buy and grow assets is probably new to you. It can also look a bit intimidating and complicated.

- Pleasure: Buying and growing assets doesn't deliver the kind of dopamine surge that would allow your primitive brain to eventually associate it with desire. The pleasure of the gains is separated in time and mostly intellectual. You can see your earnings coming in, but not typically in the "Let's take a vacation on the winnings!" kind of way.

THE ASSETS TABLE

Realizing that your job will never make you rich doesn't mean you have to quit work right away or at all. It would be very risky to get rid of your one source of support and set out in search of another. Instead, I recommend thinking of your wealth like a table which, at present, has only one or two legs. As we've already seen, the primary leg (your job) makes you entirely dependent on your employer and will never make you rich. Your second—your retirement savings accounts— are making money, but that money belongs to some future pocket, not your current one. Two legs is great for birds and people, but not tables. You need more asset legs. The more sources of income you have, the more stable your wealth table becomes. There are four primary sources of additional income. Perhaps the easiest to access is one we've already mentioned—your expertise.

CONSULTING

Many doctors, for example, do some consulting on the side or leverage their hard-won knowledge by registering to serve as expert witnesses. Are there ways within your current profession for you to diversify the way you make money? Could you offer your knowledge to others on a freelance basis or on sites like TaskRabbit? Perhaps you could teach what you know or tutor students. You could even write a book!

SIDE GIGS

Creating a side gig is another great way to build an additional source of income while simultaneously exploring other life paths or career options. Is there anything you love doing that wouldn't be a practical choice for a full-time job but that you'd enjoy spending nights and weekends on?

This could be anything from making pottery you sell online or at craft fairs to dusting off your pointe shoes and teaching ballet to kids. Is there a topic you're curious enough about that you could start a podcast about? Does your Instagram channel have enough devoted followers that you could bring in some income as an influencer? Or maybe you've always secretly really wanted to run your own business. There's probably a way you could start working on it part-time. Even if it doesn't immediately start bringing in an income, you're building value in it for the future.

INVENTION

I mentioned previously that I wouldn't suggest you drop everything to try and invent the next iPhone, but you can absolutely still create value through your own creativity. This can mean anything from starting a new business or building an online platform, to turning your career knowledge into teaching materials, inventing a new product, or putting your own spin on one that already exists.

I can already hear you arguing with me in your head with thoughts like, "Sure, I may be smart, and I certainly work hard, but I'm not creative." I get it. I used to think the same way.

Going through medical school, I was always aware of that subset of creative scientists and doctors who were innovators—inventing things or founding their own companies—but I thought they were a different breed of person. For one, they were primarily men. For another, I'd bought into the idea of creativity as something rare and special. But here's the thing: it really isn't. The biggest difference between people who create value directly "from their minds" and everyone else is, in fact, mental. It's a mindset. Creative people simply think of themselves that way and give themselves permission to follow little wisps of ideas when they pop up. They don't squash them under the weight of self-imposed limitations (and perfectionism).

If you don't think of yourself as creative and capable of bringing value into the world from your ideas, try shifting your mindset. Download some new software. It was through working with a coach that I picked up this thought upgrade. It was mind-blowing. I remember thinking, "Holy *#@!%, I can create value with my brain!" And that's just what I did. It started with my online money coaching program for female physicians and grew from there to offering group and individual coaching online and in person and now to writing books!

You can too. It's just the cultural software currently running in the world that says only very special people can get rich from the value they create in the world. This path is available to you. The only thing standing in your way is your brain.

Even while I'm encouraging you to diversify your sources of income, your brain is digging in its heels. It likes that you have just one job. One job is manageable. More—and worse, new—is scary. If your brain is arguing that you don't have the time to start consulting or launch a side gig or create value directly, recognize the objections for what they are.

INVESTING

Investing is by far the easiest and most common way of creating additional income streams. If you're funding a retirement account where you work through a 401(k), you're already participating in the stock market—probably as part of an index or mutual fund. Mutual funds operate as something of a clearinghouse or middleman between individuals and the market. Rather than buying shares in publicly traded companies yourself, you contribute to what is literally a mutually owned collection of stocks selected by the fund. This spreads out risk, allowing one or even several of the companies in your fund's portfolio to lose money without tanking everything you've saved.

You "pay" for that safety by sacrificing control. Not only do you not have a say in what stocks your fund buys, but you have no control over the behavior or performance of the companies you've paid for shares in. Of course, few of us can own a large enough percentage of a company's shares to be able to apply much pressure on its executives. Still, other investments do give you more direct control over your assets.

The other price you pay for the safety of mutual funds is the rate of interest they earn. A return of between 8 and 10 percent is typically the range you can expect to earn on these investments. People who are seeing returns on the high end of that spectrum feel pretty good about themselves, their entire investment strategy predicated on time and the power of compound interest.

While it's true that this plan will indeed make money, it makes it very slowly. Nonetheless, this is the strategy I followed for several years, although I don't anymore, and it's still the strategy I recommend to most of my clients initially.

(Now, I largely invest in real estate and even more in the last asset we're going to discuss.)

The one rule of wealth is to acquire and grow assets, so it's much more important that you begin to do this than it is to do it in the optimal way. The easiest and most accessible path is to start learning about your 401(k) accounts and what's available to you within them, but I can almost hear your primitive brain grumbling from here. It doesn't want to put more money somewhere you can't see it, where it needs to sit for years before it accrues enough interest to feel like real money. I get it. And I have a little hack for you.

TAXES

Every year at tax time (and frequently at other times when strangers learn what I do), I'm asked for tips on saving money on taxes, but this is the wrong question. Most of these people are high-income earners (most often doctors), in the top tax bracket paying taxes on a W-2. The truth is, there simply aren't many tax breaks available. There's a reason for this. The government wants tax money and sees your salary as a juicy target. Besides, you aren't generating much tax revenue for it elsewhere beyond income tax and property taxes if you own your home.

If, on the other hand, you're creating multiple tax streams for the government, it's suddenly much less interested in your income. If you own a business, you're creating jobs, and the government likes that too. If you own real estate, you're likely hiring contractors and property managers, in addition to generating property taxes. This is why business owners and real estate investors get income tax breaks.

THE BEST INVESTMENT

Taxes aren't the only thing people ask me about at parties.

I'm also regularly asked for investment tips. It's something I see in some of my clients as well. The coaching term for it is "how greed." How greed shows up as an almost manic glint in someone's eye or the familiar, "Just tell me how!" Often, they've recently had an illuminating insight into themselves or their relationships. They can now clearly see the problem that has been plaguing them for years. How can they fix it? Today, if possible.

Of course, this isn't the way people (or the market) operate. Steve Jobs didn't go out and buy a "How to Start a Computer Company" book. That doesn't keep us from falling prey to the allure of "How to X" or "Three Simple Steps to Y." I'm sure you recognize the work of your primitive brain in this. It wants someone to make it easy for you, to just tell you what to do. That said, there is one investment you can make that will never lose value. It's recession-proof, has no minimum entry price, and is guaranteed to make a difference in your quality of life. It's an investment in an asset you already own. Can you guess?

It's you.

As I mentioned above, it was during a coaching session that I recognized the hidden "I'm not creative" limitation I'd put on myself. If I hadn't, I never would have started my own business and might even still have just a two-legged wealth table. At the start of this chapter, in "Your Income Ceiling," we talked about discovering and removing unconscious limits on what you can earn. Even if that's all you get out of this chapter, the investment of your time and attention has already increased your earning potential.

Invest in Your Brain

People sometimes balk at the cost of coaching, but it's a terrific example of paying for results rather than hours. I've seen a $2,500 program completely change the trajectory of someone's life. I have a friend who spent $50,000 on a mastermind program who later told me that saying no to that initial investment in herself would have been saying no to the multimillion-dollar company she now runs. Here again, the socialization women get not to be greedy or spend money on themselves can form a formidable stumbling block. Most of us have no trouble spending multiple six figures on our kids' education, but we balk at investing in our own, especially beyond the traditional college and grad school degrees.

It can feel grandiose to invest heavily in improving your own performance or starting a company doing something you enjoy, but there are few things with better possible returns. People who are actively investing in their own businesses and contributing to the world by creating value in it almost seem to glow with energy. They no longer feel only as significant as they're paid to be. Their employers don't determine their value. They have a strong sense of purpose and direction and, even if their businesses wobble, they're frequently able to feel proud of their efforts.

Purpose, in fact, is one of several things that make life worth living. Growth is another. Even if you're not at a place in your life (or simply have no desire) to start your own business, investing in your personal growth will pay dividends in life satisfaction. Investing in your brain is betting on yourself. It's investing in an asset that will never stop yielding dividends (unless you die or something terrible happens, but that's what insurance is for!).

In Chapter 4, I said that a person's capacity to withstand feeling uncomfortable was the only limit on what was possible for them. What would happen if you got better at handling the discomfort of asking for things you wanted, of talking to someone you don't know, of failure?

FLEX YOUR MINDSET

Get creative! Brainstorm ways you can leverage your expertise, education, and specialized knowledge to create additional income streams. Shoot for ten, but don't stop until you've found at least three.

Acquiring and growing assets is the only way to become wealthy. It pays to add legs to your asset table.

A NEW DEFINITION OF INCOME

Most people impose an income ceiling on themselves without realizing they're creating limits even on what they let themselves want. These limits are often based on the incorrect belief that a salary is the only way they have to make money. But money is simply a way of measuring value, and you have more than time that's worth something. Your ability to produce results, your expertise and creativity, are all of value if you can turn them into income streams.

Understanding that money comes from value, not just from time and effort, also unlocks the one rule of wealth. Very few people get rich simply by trading time for money. They get rich by acquiring and growing assets. It's my opinion that of all the assets you can invest in, your brain is the best and safest one.

TURNING INSIGHTS INTO ACTION

1. Refer back to the Question and Answer exercise at the beginning of this chapter and reconsider how much

money you want to make. Would you like to pick a new number? Do it, then ask yourself why you made the choice you did. What are your thoughts about how much time or sacrifice (or anything else) you'd need to reach that number? Do you believe you're allowed to make that much? If not, try deliberately imagining yourself earning your new number.

2. How many legs does your asset table have? Make a list of your current asset legs. Then brainstorm additional ones to explore. List at least ten.

3. How will you invest in your brain next? In the same way that investing in your health can be as affordable as a free walk around the block and as expensive as a home gym and visiting personal trainer, there's a brain-building investment for every budget from free library books to $50,000 mastermind programs.

Old Myth: Everyone works for money. I just need to double down and work harder for longer. Eventually, I'll earn enough to make whatever I think my income ceiling is.

New Mindset: Rich people don't work for money. Because they use it to buy and grow assets, their money works for them.

Now that you have a better understanding of where wealth comes from, it's time to do the same kind of overhaul on how you think about debt.

CHAPTER 6

Myth: Debt Must Die!

I buried several common thoughts people have about debt in the "fact-finding" exercise at the top of Chapter 2. Did you mark any of them as true? Go back and take a peek if you don't remember. They're in there, in part, because of all the different reasons people give me for being stressed about money, debt is second only to "not enough." But most people don't even know what debt is.

DEBT DEFINED

Debt, like money, has no inherent moral value. Debt is not bad, and it's not wrong to have acquired some. Debt is simply money you bought. Once upon a time, there was something that you wanted that cost money. You either didn't have the money, or you had it but didn't want to spend it, so you bought some at a price we call "interest."

Most of the people I work with have a significant amount of student loan debt they're paying off, and never has one of them been happy about it. But as we saw in Chapter 2, no matter how they (or you) might feel about it, the debt isn't actually what's causing those feelings. Debt is just a number. It's a circumstance.

Many of my clients are physicians who took out loans to pay for med school, and I have a simple thought experiment that proves this point to them. I ask them to remember back to the time when they were applying to medical school—how nervous they were. How eager to become doctors. Then I have them recall how they felt when they got their acceptance letters. Sitting in my office with their eyes closed, they can't help smiling. They were so happy and proud, so ready to launch into their studies.

Then I ask how they felt about the loans. Their smiles don't even waver. Those loans were a godsend. They were delighted to get them. They were buying the money they needed to become a doctor. The money they borrowed hasn't changed. What's changed is how they think and feel about it. Now, it doesn't feel like a means to an end; it feels like a weight to carry. Worse, it's a weight heavily freighted in "shoulds." The most pervasive is that they should continue to live like a resident until they pay off all of their debt. I think this is terrible advice.

THE ONE RULE OF DEBT

In the same way that there's one rule of wealth (acquire and grow assets), there's a single rule of debt. Any extra money you put toward paying off debt is money that's not going toward acquiring and growing assets. In other words, any extra money you spend on debt subtracts from your wealth. It's pretty simple, isn't it? Even obvious. You do need to make the minimum payment on your debt, but you do not need to pay it off any faster than that. In fact, it's my argument that you probably shouldn't.

Any money you spend on low-interest debt above the minimum payment is money that's not going toward acquiring and growing assets.

This, I know, runs against conventional wisdom. It also frustrates your primitive brain. Your primitive brain likes watching the amount-owed number get smaller. Paying off debt is easy and safe. It will feel so good to be debt-free! But you know what feels better? Making money while you sleep. But not every argument in favor of aggressively paying off your student debt is equally primitive. There are two very rational-sounding ones and one that's quasi-rational. Let's take them one at a time.

STOP PAYING INTEREST

Paying off your student loans more quickly is a guaranteed return of the interest rate. In other words, if the interest is the price you're paying for the money you bought, you'll pay less for your debt the fewer days you have it. This is true as far as it goes. Yes, you'll save the 5 to 7 percent interest you're paying, but that money doesn't then start paying the interest to you. Paying off your student loans doesn't put money in your pocket.

IT'S SAFER

If something happens in the future and your income is compromised, at least you will owe less. Sure, but it's easy to put a pause on your loan if something truly major has happened, so you aren't actually saving yourself anything but a phone call.

Conventional wisdom is that it's better to be debt-free as quickly as possible. Why? I've asked everyone who's made this assertion to me, and nobody's had an answer. Sometimes they'll take the moral judgment up an additional notch with something like, "Having debt means you're bad with money," but this is simply absurd. Money has no morality. Paying off debt is neither good nor bad. The bigger takeaway is that paying off debt won't make you rich. Even once people understand this, they still struggle to prioritize buying assets over paying down debt because the primitive brain chimes in.

THIS IS YOUR BRAIN ON DEBT

In the last chapter, we looked at how the motivational triad pushes you away from accruing assets. It steers you toward paying down debt in almost a direct inverse.

As part of its "Don't Die!" strategy, your brain, which associates pleasure with eating and sex (things it wants you to do lots of), tags each pleasurable experience with dopamine so it can recognize future opportunities to repeat it. Making progress must have given our ancient ancestors enough of a survival advantage. Maybe it counterbalanced our innate laziness enough to get us to exert ourselves over longer distances to reach the next juicy berry. Either way, our brains have marked making progress with dopamine so that we get pleasure from making measurable progress toward a clear goal. This is why paying off debt feels good to the extent that it does.

It's not exactly fun to pay off debt, but there's an enjoyable righteousness to it. And your primitive brain anticipates the very good feelings it believes it will get when the debt is finally erased. It may even figure in some social recognition for its achievement if you celebrate this milestone with friends.

EASE

Paying down debt is easy, and you already know how to do it. It doesn't require you to learn anything new or to do a bunch of research. You can just click to pay.

PAIN

Since we've all been programmed that debt is bad, paying it off reduces the emotional pain of carrying it. Debt reduction gives your brain plenty of safety signals and doesn't trigger its fear about getting hurt. Not only is paying off debt unlikely to ever have direct negative consequences, but it creates an illusion of control and doesn't involve any uncertainty. You can see exactly how much you have left to pay and how much you'll "save" by paying it off early.

GOOD DEBT, BAD DEBT

When I explain one rule of debt and the reasons not to pay down more than the minimum on student loans, I inevitably get asked the good debt/bad debt question because consumer debt like high-interest credit cards is bad, right?

There is no such thing as bad debt. Debt, like money, is never good or bad. There are, however, "bad" reasons for buying money. How much debt you have is much less important than why you have it. Taking out a loan to invest in yourself is very different from taking out a loan (even a relatively low-interest loan) to buy way more car than you need. Putting the costs of starting up a new business on a credit card is not the same as charging bottles of expensive wine you don't really enjoy, trying to impress your friends.

Look carefully at the *why*, not the *how much* of your debt. Does it reveal an overdesire that's doing you financial damage? Are you buying money that you aren't then investing in something worthwhile? No matter how zealously you try to pay off your credit cards, if you have a problem with overdesire, you're going to be chasing your tail—racking up debt and paying it down over and over. Doing the work to get on top of your overdesires and dialing them down to a nonharmful level is a truly worthwhile investment that will pay off almost immediately.

DEBT STRATEGIES

For student loans, I think your best strategy is to pay only the minimum. Invest some time in exploring whether there are ways to refinance them to a lower interest rate. There usually are. Many companies are eager to buy student loan debt, so the marketplace is competitive. Also, unlike refinancing your mortgage, there are no application fees or closing costs attached and no reason not to apply to multiple offers and pit them against each other.

You can refinance your student debt at no cost
and pay less for the money you borrowed.

Negotiating lower interest rates should also be your first-line strategy for managing any consumer debt you have. If you have quite a lot, look into debt consolidation. This can sometimes drop your interest rate to as little as 3 percent, although it may tarnish your credit score for a while. Even if you have a very reasonable rate, it's almost always worth the few minutes it takes to call your credit card companies and ask for a lower one. Sometimes, asking is all it takes.

Negotiate lower interest rates on all your debt.

It makes sense to pay down any debt you're carrying that has a high (over 10 percent) interest rate before you start buying assets. There are two philosophies on how this is best done, both of which, for some reason, have very chilly names: snowball and avalanche. There is no "right" answer here. Pick the one that appeals most to you and stick with it.

AVALANCHE

To pay off debt using the avalanche model, you list out all your creditors and organize them by interest rate from highest to lowest. Let's say you owe $5,000 on your Nordstrom's store card, for example, which has a 28 percent interest rate, and you're carrying a $50,000 balance on a bank card that has a 15 percent interest rate. Let's say you also owe $500 to Home Depot, for which you're paying 9 percent. With the avalanche method, you'd pay off Nordie's $5,000 first, then the Visa's $50,000, then Home Depot's $500. Assuming you apply the same amount of money to your debt each month, this is the way to save the most money.

SNOWBALL

The snowball model is psychologically rather than mathematically based. You pay off debt from smallest to largest outstanding balance with no regard to interest rate. Using the numbers in the previous paragraph, you'd pay off Home

Depot first, then Nordstrom, and finally the Visa. The snow-ball method gives you the shortest path to the positive reinforcement of crossing debtors off your list. It also allows you to increase the amount you pay on the largest debt with each card you pay off, rolling their payments into what you're paying the remaining accounts. This rolling gathers debt-paying dollars to the largest debt lump like a snowball gathers snow.

WHERE THE MONEY COMES FROM

Once you resolve to start paying off consumer debt, there are three ways you can consider funding the payments. The first is the most obvious and, often, the only one people consider—cut expenses elsewhere. This is where the inevitable latte-sacrificing recommendation shows up. Personally, I hate doing without the things I enjoy. I don't like self-denial, budgets, or diets (more on this in the next chapter). I find I quickly begin resenting and then rebelling against any program that smacks of punishment. Remember, debt isn't bad. You're not bad for having debt, and you don't need to pay a penance for debt-sins with lattes.

If you want to take money from other places you usually spend it to pay off consumer debt, it's a solid strategy. Just be aware it's not the only one, and be careful to frame it to yourself as a temporary means to a desirable end. Think of it more like dieting the month before your sister's wedding so you'll look great in that stupid dress she picked than trying to give up cake for the rest of your life.

In addition to redirecting money to pay off debt, you can simply spend money you already have. It may seem painfully obvious, but I see a surprising number of coaching clients who have money saved that's earning a fraction of the interest they're paying on the money they owe, but they still resist using their savings to pay off their debt.

Can you guess the third way? It will seem obvious as soon as I tell you, but it's stunning how often it never occurs to people. Increase your income! Any of the multiple income streams we discussed in Chapter 5 can bring in additional income you could easily earmark for debt reduction. That way, you can pay off debt without spending your savings or giving up anything by earning more money.

A NEW DEFINITION OF DEBT

Debt is money you bought. It's neither good nor bad, but high-interest consumer debt may indicate problematic overdesires. That needs to be addressed, and the debt paid off either from the smallest amount owed to the largest in the snowball method or by tackling the highest-interest loans first in an avalanche. Whether you make those payments by cutting down on other expenses, dipping into your savings, or making more, make looking into lowering your interest rates your first step. Do this for your low-interest debt too, then pay only the minimum payment.

TURNING INSIGHTS INTO ACTION

1. When you think about your debt, what do you feel?
2. What are your thoughts (as distinct from your feelings) about debt?
3. How do you feel about taking on debt— such as investing in real estate or a new business?
4. If you have debt, make a list of everything you owe. Next to each item, write down what it was for and

recall what you were thinking and feeling when you bought the money to pay for it. How do those thoughts and feelings compare to how you think and feel now?

5. If you have debt, how do you want to think about it now? How do you want to handle it? Will you do the snowball or avalanche method—or pay the minimum so you can use your money to buy and grow assets? Make a plan and write it down.

Old Myth: Debt must die and as quickly as possible, please! I need to pay it all down as quickly as possible.

New Mindset: Killing off debt might feel good, but it won't make me rich. Only buying and growing assets can do that.

I mentioned at the top of this chapter that I'm no fan of self-denial, but I'm not arguing for overindulgence or a disregard for all moderation. I'm taking a stand against the scarcity-based thinking behind much of the traditional financial advice, including the nearly ubiquitous "Make a budget and stick to it!" In the next chapter, I'll explain why and tell you what I recommend instead.

CHAPTER 7

Myth: Budgets Are Money Diets

I hate the word "budget." I'd be willing to bet (don't bet, betting is a terrible investment) that you aren't a fan either. You probably have some experience with the idea of budgeting, though. You've probably tried several different budgeting tools, and you've probably focused on things to stop spending on, where you're going to cut back or cut out completely (there go the lattes again). It's a bit like deciding what you're going to stop eating or have only on the weekends. Budgets, like diets, tend to be very no-focused, concentrating on what we can't spend or eat and relying on willpower to deny ourselves things we enjoy. We're going to start from the opposite end.

Joy Inventory

Take a moment to think carefully about what you enjoy most. Write a list of the things in your life—whether they have anything to do with money or not—that bring you the most joy. Cuddling with your kids, spouse, or puppy? A glass of a particularly good wine at the end of the day? Road trips? Louboutins? Without any shame or guilt, write them down.

* * *

I once got an email from a woman who was interested in taking my online program. Her question boiled down to basically, "Is there a charity exemption?" She was active in several nonprofits and contributed generously to several more, and wanted some assurance that I wouldn't try to make her stop. She was proud of what her donations were helping accomplish and took a lot of personal satisfaction from it. She was confident any program that would help her "be good with money" was going to hinge on spending less. What if, I asked her, she could learn to make so much more that she increased her contributions instead? She was intrigued and joined the group, and that's exactly what ended up happening for her. Being "good with money" isn't about restricting what you spend; it's about being deliberate.

SPENDING PLANS

As you remember (I hope) from Chapter 4, willpower doesn't work. This is why most budgets (and diets) fail. People commit to no-spend months or resolve never to buy another pair of red-bottomed shoes ever again. They freeze their credit cards in blocks of ice and delete their information from their browsers. Then, almost inevitably, they "cheat" and feel bad about themselves. They've set themselves up to fail.

Spending (like pizza) isn't bad. It's just a behavior. It's a thing we do. It's time to remove the moral judgments we put on money and the blame we heap on ourselves and approach spending in a neutral way just like we did with income and debt. Rather than a restrictive budget, I recommend having a spending plan. You can make a plan for how you'll spend money without making it mean anything good or bad in the same way you'd plan a car trip or a home renovation. Because it is important to have a plan. Without one, you'll spend money unconsciously rather than deliberately.

The problem with living without a spending plan isn't necessarily that you'll spend too much (you might not spend enough). The problem is what you'll think about how you spend after you've spent it. It's hard for most smart, educated people to think highly of how they spend when their primitive brain is making all the decisions.

THIS IS YOUR BRAIN ON PLANS

Planning calls on your prefrontal cortex's uniquely human ability to anticipate the future and premake decisions that would otherwise be made in the moment by your pleasure-seeking primitive brain. Sadly, this doesn't mean, when decision time actually arrives, that your primitive brain will sleep through it. It won't.

Anyone who's gone to the grocery store hungry and without a list has had firsthand experience with the way the primitive brain shops. It shops impulsively. It shops when it's bored or wants a little hit of dopamine. As we talked about in Chapter 4, in the presence of strong overdesire, even great plans crumble, but having a spending plan in place can help you avoid a negative feedback loop.

If you don't have a plan then, (obviously) all your spending is unplanned. Unplanned spending often results in less-than-kind thoughts about that spending: "I bought a <u>what</u>? What was I thinking? God, I'm such an idiot sometimes. I'm terrible with money." Thoughts, as we know, cause feelings. The thoughts you think about some of your unplanned purchases might make you anxious or ashamed enough to need some retail therapy or make you want to stop thinking about how you spend, keeping you from making a plan for the future. Luckily, I have a simple, four-step process that makes it easy.

STEP 1: DISCOVERY

Since every good plan starts with data, we'll begin by collecting information about your money. Remember, no judgment! This is just data.

Draw a line down the center of a piece of paper and record, on one side, the places your money comes from and how much each brings in. (For most people, this is a one-item list, and that's completely fine.)

On the other side of the paper, collect what goes out each month first, in fixed amounts—your rent or mortgage, any car or student loan payments, and then in regular but "squishier" amounts—food, electricity, and other such monthly bills. Go through your credit card statements and find out what you're buying with each card. I like to gather data in broad categories: monthly fixed expenses (things like rent/mortgage, utilities), long-term expenses (items that aren't billed monthly but recur regularly like annual subscriptions or membership dues), insurances, fun spending, gifts (including charitable gifts), vacations, and of course, buying and growing assets.

STEP 2: INVESTIGATION

Once there's data, you have something to analyze. Investigate your spending. Get curious about it. There are usually some surprises during this phase, but keep your investigator's detachment. You're just learning about reality.

In Chapter 4, we talked about the net outcome of purchases. Investigate your expenses through that lens. What things did you buy that brought you joy? Are you underspending on these things? Are there purchases you made that you now regret? Where do you over-spend? If you have a scarcity mindset about money, it can show up in two almost-opposite ways as you're investigating how you spend. For some, their sense that there's never enough money makes them overly frugal. They don't spend much on anything, even less on things they enjoy, and they feel anxious about every dollar. If you're not spending money on things you know would be beneficial to you, that's a sure sign of spending from a place of scarcity.

On the other extreme of behaviors that result from scarcity thinking, there are people who spend everything they get as soon as they get it because they have no faith that more is coming. Their experience is that money doesn't stick around, so you might as well spend it while you've got it. To them, money isn't something you hold onto. It's more like grabbing fistfuls of water than filling a cistern.

If you recognize yourself in either of these scarcity mindset ways of spending, you're not alone, and there's nothing wrong with you! These are very normal ways of thinking. Our brains are wired to look for signs of scarcity, and all of us have some degree of scarcity thinking. It never goes away, but you can learn to recognize these thoughts of "not enough" for what they are—a voice in your head you don't have to believe—and start listening to them less.

STEP 3: OPTIMIZATION

In the third step of spending-plan creation, we act on what we learned in the previous two steps. As you reflect without judgment on how you've spent money in the past, think about what changes you might make to optimize for joy. Go back and look at the joy inventory you took at the start of this chapter and make sure several of the ones that cost money get into your plan. As you start assigning dollar amounts to categories, I have a few insights to offer and recommendations to make.

Have an Emergency Fund

I'm sure you've heard this advice before. Conventional wisdom is to have between three to six months of living expenses in a savings account you can easily access. But let's think this through for ourselves. What is an emergency fund for? What constitutes an emergency? For most people, the most obvious answer is job loss. However, when I ask people what they've used them for, income replacement is far from the most frequent answer. Usually, it's an unexpected and expensive home or car repair or medical bill (although I've heard a fascinating array of other answers). They all come down to this: the emergency fund has been operating as a "just in case" fund just in case there's a significant expense that isn't in the budget. That's fine, but let's put this in the plan.

Here, in the cool, judgment-free calm of optimizing our money, it's pretty obvious that if you own a car, it's going to need more than an oil change at some point. Likewise, if you own a home, you can be absolutely certain that eventually, you'll have to replace an appliance or mechanical system, paint the exterior, or fix the roof. Happily, physical breakdowns are less inevitable, but you should know what your health insurance's out-of-pocket maximum is. If your spending plan includes these possibilities, your emergency fund can be for genuinely unforeseen events.

In the realm of the unseeable, job loss is the most likely, so yes, having some money set aside in case it happens is a good idea, particularly if you're dependent on a single income stream. Now consider that saving for a possible job loss is really only something to consider if you don't have other streams of income. I recommend starting with three months of expenses. Later, you can consider expanding to six. Notice I didn't say "income." Your expenses, I hope, are lower than your income, and that's what you'll need while you're looking for a new job.

As an example, let's say you work in a field where layoffs are frequent, so you want to have enough squirreled away to cover your expenses for five months—let's say that amounts to $15,000. That's just to cover your daily living expenses, not any unexpected home repairs or medical bills, so you'll want to have some money saved for those things too. Let's make it easy and say that's another $15,000 in case someone gets sick or you need to replace the water heater. Where are you going to keep this $30,000?

The answer (short of mason jars in the yard) is whatever makes you feel safe. Everyone has a different tolerance for risk (more on this in the next section); just make your choice strategically. Don't default into the typical separate savings account at your bank. Yes, keep your emergency fund there if that's what makes you feel safe, but these accounts earn below the rate of inflation in interest. (And don't waste your time searching for the bank with the highest savings rate;

they're all low single digits, and the difference between the best and the worst is less than the cost of a latte.)

I recommend keeping just a month or two's expenses in your regular checking account and investing the rest of your emergency fund in a traditional brokerage account. If you need it, that money can be in your checking account in less than a week. You simply sell your shares (or some portion of them) and transfer the proceeds. For people who own a home, the ability to tap into its equity can substitute for maintaining an emergency fund.

Make Debt a Line Item

We've already talked quite a lot about debt, and by now you know my stance on aggressively paying off low-interest loans (don't). That said, if you have minimum monthly payments on student loans, do make sure they're in your spending plan. Also, if you're convinced you'd feel better with them gone and want to pay them off as quickly as you can, make a plan for that too. Finally, if you're paying over 10 percent in interest on any loans, make a plan to get rid of that as quickly as you can.

Avoid planning to spend too much on debt out of a misplaced sense of virtue. Planning to give up everything you enjoy until you're out of even your high-interest consumer debt is like vowing to give up sugar until you're back in your high school jeans. You're as likely to end up adding to what you're trying to shed as you are to actually get rid of debts (or inches).

Automate What You Can

I don't actually "pay bills" every month. I've enabled autopay for every regular monthly expense I have, and I recommend you do the same. Even if you're planning to pay off your credit card bill every month, set up an autopay for the minimum. It's maddening to have to pay a late fee because you forgot one month or were on vacation when the bill came.

Make It Monthly

In addition to the unpleasant not-really-unexpected-but-unplanned expenses covered by the "just in case" fund, you probably have expenses that happen less frequently than once a month but are still predictable. Maybe you take an annual vacation, for example, or love to pull out all the stops at Christmas, or attend conferences, or invest in your own development through education, coaching, or workshops (this is often a category where people find they're under-spending when they conduct a joy audit). Make a plan for which nonmonthly things you'll do and guestimate what they're likely to cost. Divide that number by twelve and add it to your spending plan. You won't be spending that line item down to zero every month, but you will be spending it!

Think Sand, Not Stone

As you start to allocate dollar amounts to line items, keep in mind that what you're creating is a draft. You're unlikely to get it right on your first go. This isn't a once-and-done, fix-everything-now process. (Wave to your Chapter 3 perfectionism as you put it back to bed.) Nothing here is written in stone. You will probably end up moving dollar amounts around. You may even add new line items.

STEP 4: IMPLEMENTATION

Once you have a plan, it's time to take it out into the world for a test drive. This will be less like heading down to your local

Honda dealership and more like the test drives Orville and Wilbur Wright took off of sand dunes. The point is less about your plan's relative "success" than it is about the learnings each month's experiment yields. Review your plan and compare it against reality no less than once a month, but weekly or biweekly is even better (especially as you start out).

Each of these reviews is a miniaturized version of the entire process: gather the most recent income and outflow numbers, assess your spending on the joy-regret scale, optimize your spending plan, and put the new one into practice. Try to do all this with a scientist's detachment—observing and experimenting with no more judgment than you'd have about the performance of a bacteria culture.

NEW PROGRAMS

Since we've talked about downloading new software for your brain, let me clarify that here, I'm speaking literally. If you've done much googling about money, debt, or budgeting, you've probably seen ads for programs like Mint and Quicken. They can be helpful, but most of them are entirely backward-looking. Obviously, it's important to know how you've spent in the past, but it'd be much more useful to be able to look ahead into the future. (I always think about this ability as being like the precogs in the movie *Minority Report*.)

One program that does this is called YNAB and I like it even though the "b" of its acronym name is for "budget," as in You Need a Budget. It's very forward-focused and helps people make predictions about future spending. There are probably other budget forecasting programs out there, and YNAB has a steep learning curve, so I encourage you to do your own research and experiment to find out what's best for you and your goal of optimizing your spending plan.

A NEW DEFINITION OF BUDGETING

Budgets are too often about self-denial and rigid rules we set for ourselves. They smack of judgment and calls for will-power, and they are more likely to make us swing from rebellion to compliance and back again. Planning, on the other hand, leverages the unique abilities of our prefrontal cortex to premake decisions based on a metric of joy. By taking the time to discover and investigate how we spend and to create and then implement a plan that optimizes future spending, we not only take more control of our finances, but we spend more on the things that bring us the most joy.

TURNING INSIGHTS INTO ACTION

1. Take a moment to think carefully about what you enjoy most. Write a list of the things in your life—whether they have anything to do with money or not—that bring you the most joy.
2. Create your spending plan using the four steps outlined in this chapter. The free downloadable companion PDF workbook I've created will be particularly helpful for this. Get it here: definingwealthforwomen.com. I also recommend the app YNAB (You Need A Budget) for creating and implementing spending plans.

Old Myth: Budgets are money diets. I just need to buckle down and tighten my belt.

New Mindset: Creating a spending plan will help me understand how I've spent money in the past and make decisions about how I want to spend it in the future to optimize for joy.

Does the idea of a more joy-filled life create some kind of resistance in you? In Chapter 5, we talked about the tendency for some women to put an income ceiling on their desire for a larger income. Do you have a happiness threshold? Do you have a (perhaps previously unrecognized) belief that life isn't supposed to be full of joy? In the next chapter, we'll take a closer look at what reality is actually like.

CHAPTER 8

Myth: Life Is Just That Way

A few months ago, I got a long letter from Susan, a young female physician who'd just finished her residency the year before. After so much debt and so many years of school and residency to become a board-certified attending, she had finally arrived. For almost a year, she'd been living the life she'd worked so hard to achieve, and she wasn't loving it.

She didn't hate being a doctor, she explained, but she did hate how scared and disappointed she felt that she wasn't as happy as she'd expected to be. She'd followed all the rules and succeeded at everything she'd set out to do—so why did she feel like she'd failed?

She had a friend from med school who'd recently pivoted and was starting her own company, but Susan felt like she couldn't possibly throw it all away and pursue a different goal. What if the same thing happened when she reached it?

What if she just wasn't good at happiness? What if life was just that way?

That, when I got right down to it, was what she was writing me to ask: was she just being a child who needed to grow up and accept that life was just like that?

Reality Check

Mark each of the statements below with an "H" if you've heard them before from your parents, your teachers, or your friends. Add an "A" to the ones you agree with.

Life isn't fair.

Life is hard.

Life is short.

Life's an experiment.

If you work hard, you'll do well.

If you stand out, you'll get cut down.

You need to start saving for retirement while you're still young.

---

* * *

By now, it should come as no surprise that we get many of our ideas about what we expect life to be like not from reality, but from what our parents, culture, and mindset have made reality mean. There are certain things that are true of life. There are (forgive me) facts of life, but we often pay less attention to them than we do to opinions we didn't necessarily even decide on for ourselves. Susan said she'd followed the rules, but whose rules was she talking about? Are they based on truths about the world or someone else's opinion?

Most likely they're not even rules, and what Susan meant when she said she'd followed them was that she'd followed the social norms she was raised with. This, as with everything else we've discussed, isn't good or bad, but it is a choice—or it can be. To understand our options better, we need to take a closer look at two submyths of the myth that life is just the way we've been told it is.

In Chapter 6, I mentioned the way our current school system was established by the leaders of the Industrial Revolution to train children to follow the rules of factory work and to develop the skills it valued: obedience, rule following, showing up on time, and focusing on one task at a time for long periods. Curiosity, critical thinking, and a love of learning were not only not valued, but they created a hindrance and were actively discouraged.

These industrialists designed our free, mandatory education to shape anyone who wasn't wealthy (and everyone who wasn't white or male) into uniformly sized, interchangeable parts that fit neatly into the factories they ran. To maximize its profits on these human resources, those factories needed people to work regular hours on reliable schedules with a minimum of disruption for the maximum number of years they were serviceable. In other words, the industrial economy needed to structure people's time into eight-hour days in five-day weeks for forty-eight to fifty weeks of the year for thirty or forty years. In exchange for what? Retirement—the promise of eventually getting to do whatever we want with however much time we have left.

MYTH: LIFE BEGINS AT RETIREMENT

To fund that distant freedom, we're advised to dutifully start saving as soon as possible and investing our savings in index or mutual funds earning as much as 10 percent. This, we're told, through the miracle of compound interest, will support our lifestyle in our old age. But who decided 10 percent is the upper limit of what we should expect our investments to return? For that matter, who decided we needed to wait decades to own our own time? And why do so many of us believe and follow it? Because that's what we were taught when we were children and couldn't think for ourselves. Because even if we hadn't been, this system's core values are so deeply woven into the fabric of our society that there's no way we could have escaped being socialized to them.

THE CULT OF PRODUCTIVITY

In Chapter 5, I challenged the widely accepted (if largely unacknowledged) belief that the only way of creating value is to trade time or effort for money. Under that model, to earn more, you need to either work more hours or work harder during the hours you work—and probably both. Because the number of hours in a day is finite and the same for everyone, people have focused on the second half of this limited equation, trying to do more in less time—in other words, on productivity.

Productivity was the driving idea behind the rise of factories in the Industrial Revolution. It's as though everyone simply missed that men (yes, just men) like Henry Ford created value from the idea of a new mode of manufacture as much as from the productivity it enabled.

> Interestingly, Mr. Ford himself seems to have been clued into the much richer, if less obvious, source of value. He apparently paid a man $50,000 (that's $750,000 in today's dollars adjusted for inflation) to sit in an office down the hall with his feet up on his desk. When challenged by a business consultant, Ford apparently justified it by saying that a few years earlier, the man had come up with an idea that saved Ford $2 million with his feet in pretty much the same place.

Productivity is a key tenant of the Protestant work ethic, and Celeste Headlee, the author of Do Nothing, identifies the same drive for ever-increasing productivity as the reason so many of us are "working more instead of less, living harder, not smarter, and becoming more lonely and anxious." Still, the quest for productivity is baked into capitalism in particular and Western culture in general. Both Christianity and Judaism explicitly warn against idleness, reserving even rest for once a week and setting up the idea that leisure is for after all the day's work is done. For men, this used to mean sundown. For women, it's always meant never.

This institutional sexism only got worse as "work" came to mean "work done for money," making all labor involved in running a home and raising children not only unpaid and without (economic) value but also not really work. Loading a lifetime's work into the young years and saving leisure for retirement isn't just an artificial construct, then; it's also inherently sexist.

Recently, a new movement called FIRE (Financial Independence, Retire Early) has doubled down on the central promise of our cultural obsession with productivity. As its name suggests, FIRE is basically a time-compressed version of the "wait for retirement to enjoy life" ethic it claims to replace. It recommends working much harder for even fewer years and maximizing your productivity to get to the good stuff of not working more quickly. The core idea, however, is the same— work comes from time and effort, and not having to do it anymore is the only way to enjoy life.

What FIRE (and indeed pretty much the entire "Life Begins at Retirement" myth) misses is that retiring to a life of leisure is very rarely as satisfying as people expect it to be. The basic premise ignores the way humans understand time and doesn't stand up to scrutiny under Chapter 2's emotion model (thoughts, not circumstances, determine how we feel) or even to critical thinking's breakdown of the arrival fallacy.

THIS IS YOUR BRAIN ON TIME

We've already talked about the way the primitive brain doesn't understand the future costs of present actions, but human beings, like most animals, do have a kind of internal clock that syncs with (and is probably derived from) the natural world. It breaks time into days (from one sunrise to the next), months (from one new moon to the next), and years (from one spring to the next). Most humans in most civilizations have lived in fundamental harmony with these increments of time. Nowhere in that system is there a reason for a forty-hour workweek lived for a two-day weekend or a forty-year work life followed by a work-free retirement.

We simply aren't designed to work that hard for that long— day-to-day or hour-to-hour. In fact, many of the most successful women I know work three days a week, reserving the rest of their time for the kinds of leisure and play that rejuvenate their minds and fuel their creativity.

Thinking is phenomenally energy intensive. We simply aren't biologically capable of sustained focus and attention for much longer than ninety minutes at a stretch. Nevertheless, today's knowledge workers are expected to work the same eight-hour day made standard for factory workers.

THE ARRIVAL FALLACY

The work-save-retire model is based on the idea that the joys of retirement make a lifetime of work worthwhile. We're encouraged to postpone today's happiness for tomorrow's because we'll be happy once we retire. This kind of "I'll be happy when" thinking is a great example of the same kind of arrival fallacy that got Susan through twenty-five years of formal education (and into $200,000 of debt). She'd worked as hard as she did and believed that once she was a doctor, she'd be happy.

The arrival fallacy is a fallacy because circumstances—being a doctor, being retired—aren't capable of making us happy. Or fulfilled or proud of ourselves. Circumstances don't cause feelings. Thoughts do, and we tend to take our thoughts with us as we move from circumstance to circumstance. Having arrived at her goal of becoming a board-certified doctor, Susan was still thinking about happiness as a state caused by something outside herself.

She felt disappointed because she thought she should feel differently than she did once she got where she'd been going. She felt frightened because she had thought she'd done everything right. She'd followed the rules. She had gone to school and worked hard. She'd held up her end of the deal, and life had failed to deliver. If she couldn't trust conventional wisdom to keep her safe, what could she count on?

What keeps the "life begins at retirement" myth humming (or limping) along is the pain-avoidance leg of the triangle. Susan went along with the culturally accepted story of working hard, saving up, and retiring because she believed what she'd been told about the risks of doing otherwise. She's not alone.

MYTH: RISK IS RISKY

Many of the people who work full-time for companies do so in the name of job security. We're told the gig economy and entrepreneurship are risky—your job might just evaporate. But no job is secure. We can't predict the future. There's no certainty that your full-time job will be there in a year, and your employer (probably) has no contractual obligation to you anyway.

The desire to avoid risk is also behind the investment strategy that conventional wisdom favors for funding retirement. We're taught to put our retirement savings into mutual or index funds, counting on compound interest and the very long time that money is held in savings to counter the extremely low interest rate. Any other strategy, we're told, is just too risky. But here's the secret—and it isn't even secret—nobody gets rich by playing it safe. In fact, most rich people have lost a lot of money because the kind of risks that have made them rich don't always work out.

THIS IS YOUR BRAIN ON RISK

As I mentioned in Chapter 5, the glacial speed of the progress made accumulating wealth through the power of compound interest isn't enough to create much of a dopamine surge.

Nevertheless, most of us still manage to save some for retirement in the "safe" index and mutual funds that return between 8 and 10 percent. This slow progress ekes out a bit of dopamine. More importantly, it stays below the threshold of the fear response that makes us avoid things our brain thinks will cause pain. Riskier investments run smack into it. For most people, the fear of losing money is much stronger than the pleasure derived from making progress in its accumulation. There are several reasons for this. In Chapter 2, I talked about the "under a bridge" fear that many of my clients express. This fear shows the very close link people have with losing money and real, physical danger. Yes, in an economy where money is the only way to provide for our most basic needs, losing everything can have life-and-death consequences. It usually doesn't, and very few of us ever even approach actually losing everything. Still, our fear of losing money is, on some level, a primal fear.

It's also a social one.

Friendships and belonging feel good, and social shame and exclusion feel bad because living in groups once kept us safer from predators than if we were on our own. We're exquisitely sensitive to our place in the tribe hierarchy (our social status) because it was once a life-and-death metric. The fear of losing status and the protection of our clan is behind our fear of failure.

Of course, if we really loved ourselves and completely accepted ourselves for who we were as we were, we wouldn't need external validation to prop up a faltering self-opinion. But although very few of us actually risk being rejected by our family and peers if our investments lose money or our new business venture fails, most of us also don't have that level of self-regard. The fear of failure is added to or made to mean the same thing as a fear of losing money.

WHAT FAILURE IS

Most people are so upset by the idea of failure that they struggle to define it. Take a moment and think for yourself—what does failure mean?

It means this: failure is getting an outcome you didn't want.

Life is an experiment. We formulate a hypothesis ("I'll be happy when I'm a doctor"; "I'll make money if I buy this stock"), then we act on it. When we either do or don't get the outcome we expected, we tell ourselves a story about what happened. But what if we simply adjusted our hypothesis and tried something else? Failure isn't immoral. It isn't bad, and you aren't going to get kicked out of the tribe. There's no reason for shame. Failure is data. And that's all it is.

Failure is feedback.

Most of my clients are highly educated achievers who don't have a lot of experience with failure. Perhaps if they'd had more, the thoughts they have about it that make them anxious wouldn't be quite so dire. They'd know from experience that they could bounce back from failure. Often, there's a feedback loop where their terror of failure prevents them from getting much practice failing, which increases their fear.

If this sounds like you, it's not your fault. Our school system and much of our cultural morality have given us a lot of strong messaging about fear. "Bad" students fail. If you fail an exam, you didn't work hard enough. We're taught that failure is avoidable if you follow the rules and that it should be avoided because it means you've done something wrong. But it doesn't. You didn't get the outcome you were hoping to get. You've nonetheless conducted a successful experiment because you did get an outcome.

All too often, we make "failure" mean something about who we are and what we're worth as people. Rather than seeing it as something that happened, we see it as saying something about our identity. We think "I'm such a loser!" instead of "I lost" and "There's something wrong with me" rather than "Something went wrong." It can seem like a subtle distinction, but there's a weight of shame that goes with the one that putting some distance between who you are and what outcome you get eliminates (or at least lessens). Nobody enjoys failure, and it's fine to feel sad or disappointed when you don't get what you want, but that's very different from diving into the shame spiral of being sad about who you are and disappointed with yourself!

Honestly, running the same "successful" experiment over and over isn't success. Sure, if you're "testing" facts rather than guesses, you'll avoid getting anything but the expected outcome, but that's not how learning and progress happen.

If you've ever watched a child learn to walk, you've seen experiential learning in action. And I'll bet you didn't judge that baby for falling down—for failing to walk—nor did the baby dust itself off with a grumbled, "Well, I won't try that again!"

As a doctor, I've been in situations where mistakes could be fatal. Certainly, when you have someone else's life quite literally in your hands, you want to be very careful. No matter how much it may feel that way, you aren't risking your life when you start a new business or put money into real estate or take a mini-retirement now rather than saving up all your leisure time for the end of your life. It's the decoupling of these beliefs that allows many rich people to take the kind of risks that made them rich. They don't look at losing money as failing but as part of the process of making more.

Making more money, in turn, frees them up to think less about money and more about the things (and value) they want to create in the world. Because they're worrying less about their finances, they're reserving their brain time to be more creative. They're more able to approach life (and money) from an abundance rather than a scarcity mindset, investing in those things they find meaningful and which contribute to their sense of purpose in life.

BECOME WILLING TO LOSE MONEY

In Chapter 1, you learned that your mindset can remove or introduce whole new realms of experience and possibility. In Chapter 2, I explained that thoughts, not events or circumstances, cause emotions. Putting those ideas together, I'd like to suggest that if you can develop a mindset that sees failure as feedback and serves up thoughts that affirm your safety when your primitive brain starts screaming its fear of losing money, you can start using your prefrontal cortex to take smart risks that offer the chance at much higher rewards.

The secret to getting rich is being able to deal with the emotional discomfort of losing money. I call this secret skill "wealth confidence" and define it as the ability to experience all your feelings and fully trust yourself. If you're not willing to fail, you'll never be willing to try. If you don't try, you'll never succeed. You miss 100 percent of the shots you don't take.

Because being willing to lose money doesn't mean you're going to enjoy it when it happens, and because having a few techniques for handling failure can make it easier to take the risk in the first place, I want to share with you a few of the ways I talk to myself about risk and failure.

I take pride in having walked into the arena. I remind myself that I'm not living my life sitting on the sidelines and that when you're in the game, you're taking the risk of being knocked off your feet.

I get curious about what each experience has taught me. Some coaches recommend looking at each experience as something that has happened *for* (rather than to) you, but I find that recommendation can be annoying. Instead, I ask myself: "What is this preparing me for? What admission fee did I just pay with that difficult experience? What insights did I learn?"

I also like to look at where else I'm winning. One of the upsides of the social expectation that women will participate in more than just one domain—that we will have social and domestic lives as well as economic ones—is that even when I suffer a blow in one area, I'm usually doing okay in a couple others.

Earlier in this chapter, I introduced you to another way I think about things when I don't get the result I wanted—and sometimes even when I do. It's asking the question, "Who says?" Who says 8 to 10 percent is what we should expect as a return on investments? Who says we have to work for thirty to forty years in the field we went to school for? Yes, our brains like easy, and it's easier to go along with conventional wisdom than to head out to make some wisdom of our own, but I don't think you'd still be reading if you didn't already know it's worth it.

BECAUSE YOU SAY SO

We've already talked about why women are often more attuned to and dependent on other people's good opinion of us. We're also subject to more expectations. Men are socialized to be successful at their jobs. Women are too. We're also expected to marry and have children (in that order, thank you!) and to take care of our bodies and faces, our parents and friends. We can have a choice if we take the time to make it. That choice making starts with asking ourselves questions about what matters most to us, what we want to have and do, and how we want to live and interact. Ask yourself, what does "rich" mean to you? What do you want "work" and "retirement" to look like? How comfortable are you with feeling uncomfortable? What would an increased tolerance for discomfort perhaps make possible?

Ask the big questions.

In Chapter 7, we talked about making a spending plan. The same thing that increases your awareness of and control over your spending works for the rest of your life. Still, as Michael Hyatt, author of *Free to Focus*, has observed, most people spend more time planning a vacation than they do planning their life. We're so often so busy on the hamster wheel of getting things done, running furiously (we think) toward what will make us happy, that we don't slow down and back up enough to see we're not getting anywhere. In Chapter 5, I asked you how much you wanted to make. Now, I'm suggesting you stop running long enough to ask yourself what you want to do with it.

A NEW DEFINITION OF REALITY

Many of the things we believe are "just that way" about work and time are legacies left over from the Industrial Age. They aren't inevitable. They're just opinions, not facts, and often ignore or run counter to the actual truths of our human brains. We follow the rules and fall victim to the cult of productivity, believing it will keep us safe. But once again, you can bring your more evolved prefrontal cortex to bear on your primitive brain and understand that failure is simply not getting the outcome you wanted in one of your life experiences.

The more you can learn to simply allow your uncomfortable feelings, the more you become willing to take the kind of risks that create wealth. Our fear and society's rules may "program" us to accept that reality is "just that way." But it isn't. Life is only and exactly the way you decide it is. It begins whenever you decide it does, and risk isn't risky. Life is risky. No job is secure, and no investment is loss proof (with the possible exception of your own mind). Take the time to ask yourself the big questions. Define your own life.

TURNING INSIGHTS INTO ACTION

1. Carve out some time to think about and plan your life. What do you want it to look like? Does it include continuing to work five days a week with only a few weeks of vacation a year?

2. Think back to the last time you "failed." Write down how you felt. What did you make the failure mean? Did you make it mean something about you?

3. How do you want to think and feel about failure from now on? (You may want to refer back to Chapter 4 and review how to process feelings.) What would be different in your life if you learned to process and release your disappointment about not getting the outcomes you want?

4. Are you up for the challenge of learning how to feel discomfort (in taking risks) to create and live the life of your dreams? Why or why not?

Old Myth: Life begins at retirement, and risk is risky. That's just the way it is. I need to stop hoping for more and keep myself safe by following the rules and avoiding (or at least trying to avoid) taking any big risks.

New Mindset: No one ever got rich playing it safe. I'm going to figure out what wealth means for me and start creating it!

CONCLUSION

I want you to be wealthy. I want you to experience life fully—with peace, purpose, and plenty of cash!

Why? Because wealth isn't something that's reserved for the lucky few. It's available to you. As more women become wealthy, we create examples not only for ourselves, but for our daughters and their daughters; and our sons grow up knowing that women can be rich. In other words, as we get wealthy, we rewrite history.

Creating a new money mindset isn't easy. Your primitive brain will try to hold you back. But the more you invest in your brain, the stronger your prefrontal cortex gets. This process starts with challenging what you've always believed about money, the cultural narrative about how women should (and should not be) around money, and the societal norm that debt is bad.

It continues with building your Wealth Confidence—your ability to fully trust yourself and experience all your feelings. This includes increasing your capacity to enjoy your life now rather than waiting for retirement to reap the fruits of a lifetime of labor, becoming more comfortable with allowing difficult feelings, and starting to take more self-affirming risks. After all, it's riskier *not* to take risks!

The more this new, more expansive, empowering, and enriching way of thinking and feeling becomes second nature, the less you'll need to think about money, and the more you'll be able to invest in the things that keep contributing to your peace, your purpose, and your wealth.

Remember, you are meant to be wealthy.

I believe you can. I believe all women can.

ACKNOWLEDGEMENTS

B irthing a book truly takes a whole village.

To Matt, my partner in life, love, and parenting. Thank you for always believing in and supporting me.

To my baby Jack, I love being your mother and I love that you will grow up with strong examples of wealthy women. I love you so much.

To my bonus son Wren, thank you for allowing me to be part of your family.

To Mom, my first example of a smart woman. Thank you for everything.

To my team at Scribe Media—Skyler Gray, Mikey Kershisnik, (and many others!) This book would not have been possible without you!

To Cindy Bae, for encouraging me to start.

To my first coach, Sunny Smith, who dared me to create an impossible wealth goal and instilled the belief that maybe, just maybe, I could do it.

To Peter Kim, for daring me to go big or go home.

To Letizia Alto and Kenji Asakura, for encouraging me and countless others to create financial freedom.

To Brooke Castillo, for being an example of a woman with wealth unapologetically.

To my business coach and mentor, Stacey Boehman, for allowing me to dream bigger than I could ever imagine, for being my example of a woman who can create lots of wealth and live life to the fullest, for questioning the status quo of women and wealth, and for creating the room with 100-plus millionaires.

To all the coaches in the 200K mastermind and 2 million dollar group, for inspiring me and being the best business community one could ever ask for.

To Kara Loewentheil, for opening my eyes to the history and socialization of women and for being a relentless champion of women embodying their best selves.

To the women in Money for Women Physicians, you've inspired and moved me with your daring greatly.

To all women physicians for being the inspiration for what I do and for being some of the most dedicated people on this planet. I salute you. It is an honor to be among you.

To everyone else who has ever believed in me and my ideas, thank you. I received it. Thank you for believing in me.

ABOUT THE AUTHOR

Bonnie Koo, MD, is a wealth coach, physician, and the founder of Wealthy Mom MD. Her mission is to teach and empower women with the cognitive tools to create wealth.

While facing her own financial struggles after completing her medical degree at Columbia, Bonnie decided to educate herself and make her money work for her. Today, she's a CEO and thought leader on the topic of wealth for women.

When she's not coaching, speaking, or podcasting, you can find Bonnie chasing her toddler son or under an umbrella in Hawai'i.

To learn more about Bonnie and creating the wealth you want, go to wealthymommd.com and subscribe to the *Wealthy Mom MD* podcast.

BE A PART OF THE WOMEN'S WEALTH REVOLUTION

Join the women's wealth revolution and contribute your voice to the ongoing conversation by going to wealthymommd.com and subscribing to the *Wealthy Mom MD* podcast.

There you can find more information about my coaching programs (online and in person) such as Money for Women Physicians, my signature program for wealth creation for women physicians.

Be sure to go to definingwealthforwomen.com to download your free PDF workbook to accompany this book.

I wish you wealth as we've defined it for women—peace, purpose, and plenty of cash!